STEPHEN GAMBLE

# VISUAL

# CONTENT

# MARKETING

Leveraging **Infographics**, **Video**, and **Interactive Media**
to Attract and Engage Customers

Cover image: Kittisak_Taramas
Cover design: Wiley

This book is printed on acid-free paper.

Published by John Wiley & Sons, Inc., Hoboken, New Jersey
Published simultaneously in Canada

For general information about our other products and services, please contact our Customer Care Department within the United States at (800) 762-2974, outside the United States at (317) 572-3993 or fax (317) 572-4002.

Wiley publishes in a variety of print and electronic formats and by print-on-demand. Some material included with standard print versions of this book may not be included in e-books or in print-on-demand. If this book refers to media such as a CD or DVD that is not included in the version you purchased, you may download this material at http://booksupport.wiley.com. For more information about Wiley products, visit www.wiley.com.

**Library of Congress Cataloging-in-Publication Data is available.**

Printed in the United States of America

10  9  8  7  6  5  4  3  2  1

# CONTENTS

## PART 3 — SHOWCASE OF VISUAL SOLUTIONS

### VISUAL SOLUTIONS IN BUSINESS ACTION

### INFOGRAPHICS

### INBOUND MARKETING PROGRAMS

### VIDEO

### SOLUTION PICTOGRAMS

### INTERACTIVE SOLUTION PICTOGRAMS

### DATA-DRIVEN VISUALIZATIONS AND APPLICATIONS

## IDEATION AND PRODUCT DEVELOPMENT INDUSTRY VISUAL SOLUTIONS

## IT/NETWORKING INDUSTRY VISUAL SOLUTIONS

## MANAGEMENT CONSULTING INDUSTRY VISUAL SOLUTIONS

## MEDIA INDUSTRY VISUAL SOUTIONS

## PHARMACEUTICAL INDUSTRY VISUAL SOLUTIONS

## PROFESSIONAL SERVICES INDUSTRY VISUAL SOLUTIONS

## RESEARCH INDUSTRY VISUAL SOLUTIONS

# ACKNOWLEDGEMENTS

I would like to start with my family and my mother, Betty, and my father, Fred, for laying the foundation for me to pursue my career and passions wherever they may lie. I would like to thank my son, Adrian, for always being a sounding board and always bringing his keen intellect to whatever point intellectually or professionally I might be advancing. And for my three-year-old son—Dylan—I'm thankful that he brings a sense of wonderment as we tackle life's big problems like whether a dinosaur is stronger than a tiger. I would like to thank Dean Proessell, who in my philosophy graduate days drove me into the deeper waters of issues around philosophy of language and metaphysics over extended and spirited debate tables at our local coffee shop. I would like to thank Peter Bulko, who introduced me to the complex world of technology and Wall Street and softened my entrance to the nuanced layers of technical applications and business functions as well as the corridors of Manhattan itself. I would like to thank Joseph Singh, with whom I have had the opportunity to work along side of at three companies and to learn the fine craft of consulting and the difficult path of navigating professional services delivery with go-to market excellence.

And finally, I would like to thank Katerina who, besides providing me the privilege of being her life partner, has been a steady rock in making Frame Concepts operational and a sounding board for every new idea we come up with in the always changing adventure of tackling pressing business communication challenges with visual solutions.

# ABOUT THE AUTHOR

For the last six years, Stephen Gamble, as the founder and CEO of Frame Concepts, has been solving the most pressing business communication challenges for some of the most complex offerings in the world. Stephen began his career as a mechanical engineering technologist in the 1980s and returned to complete a master's degree and doctorial studies in philosophy, focusing on philosophy of language issues as well as teaching philosophy and business subjects at City University of New York and the Metropolitan College of New York.

Stephen returned to the business world as lead corporate trainer in a large marketing agency in the 1990s and then focused on technical communications and marketing financial applications in Wall Street. Stephen jumped head first into the fresh startup movement in the late 1990s into the 2000s as the lead marketing resource and chief marketing officer for a wide array of technology startups that focused on a wide range of challenging and technical subject areas, including Linux-based operating systems, global IT lifecycle management, electronic bill presentment and payment, meta-data architecture, mobile trading applications, cross channel social marketing applications, B2C and B2B ecommerce platforms, cross-border data privacy, information lifecycle management, and business intelligence solutions. In all of Stephen's career and academic experiences, he has been in the trenches face-to-face with the burden of explaining dense and complex subject matter and provoking audiences to engage with a point of view or offering being advanced. Such wide and deep experiences makes Stephen uniquely poised to write this book.

# ABOUT THE CONTENT

The content of this book in layered in three parts. **Part 1** presents argumentation that there is in fact a business communication challenge and information design and that visual solutions are the most effective way to overcome these challenges. The arguments presented in Part 1 are partly to convince the reader about the viability of visual solutions. However, given that the reader has purchased this book, he or she may already be a visual solution convert and is looking for a sustained argument to overcome management and the budget office to enable his or her organization to leverage visual solutions.

**Part 2** assumes everyone is onboard with a visual solution and provides practical advice on the different type of visual solution providers, how to scope in the projects, and how to manage the creative process.

**Part 3** is a visual showcase to show through example how a variety of industries, professions, and organizations are putting visual solutions into action. The hope is that it may drive ideas for their own practices and also be a compelling argument, in light of its sheer magnitude, that visual solutions have a part to play in business communications.

# ABOUT FRAME CONCEPTS

All of the visual samples in this book were created by Frame Concepts, so I thought it made sense to say a word or two about Frame Concepts. Frame Concepts is a visual solution agency formed in 2010 by the author of this book. It boasts arguably the most comprehensive suite of visual solutions dedicated purely for business communications. At first it focused on infographics, but quickly spread to interactive solutions, process pictograms, and animated infographics. It then blossomed into data driven applications, including a nuclear spare parts visualization tool, a global financial interactive risk map, and a multimedia interactive Accounting Association timeline, to mention a few.

Frame Concepts' product road map is driven by ideation and actual client need and so quickly adapted all its visual solutions to enable all the classic marketing and training communication agency tools, including websites, marketing automation programs, client performance dashboards, interactive training tools, case studies, infographic rich media unit banner advertisements, transformation vision maps, and integrated film and animated infographic case studies, among others.

Regardless of the complexity of the subject matter or the technical medium that Frame Concepts deploys, the project always starts with a blank page and then a pencil sketch. The star of the show is information design, resolving the fundamental issue of how a complex issue can be made intuitive and engaging with a visual that fits on the back of a cereal box. Once that nut is cracked, then creative and technical execution see it through to the application that the client needs with the client's particular interfaces with its own clients, marketplace, and employees.

So while Frame Concepts creates some of the most rigorous visual solutions in the world on very nuanced subject matter, the problem is solved with a pencil and a piece of paper and adept use of information design principles.

# DEDICATION

I would like to dedicate this book
to whoever is or had been placed
in a role where an exciting offering
or approach is in play but nobody,
including your clients, the marketplace, and perhaps even the staff,
is "getting it." You are not alone,
and this book is your rallying cry
and plan and inspiration to get your
audience to a point of understanding and engagement.

# FOREWORD

Sometimes the stars do align, and when the publisher's editorial team approached me to write this book, I was five years in at Frame Concepts and had tested my conviction that visuals can indeed solve challenging business communication problems through actual client project delivery. Coincidently, I was forming my thoughts on this in the form of a speaking presentation and also some thought leadership with an infographic series on the topic—using infographics to talk about the effectiveness of infographics. So all the ingredients to write the book were in play.

But more importantly, my 20 years or so on the client side before forming the Frame Concepts visual solution agency was really the motivation for the book. It is the book I wish I had had as I struggled to use clever copy and stock photos and graphic and web design to explain and engage my audiences on subtle and complex subject matter and offerings. The importance and the timeliness of this book are driven by a casual glance around at even cutting-edge businesses' websites, marketing materials, and sales presentations. By and large, they are still a throwback to the attempt to look professional with stylized photos and catchy tag lines, but when you try to come to terms with the solution, you are forced to pore through dense and lengthy text. While we at Frame Concepts are remedying this issue on a daily basis, there is still a mountain of business communication problems waiting for visual packaging enabled by the information design craft.

In 2016, we will see a mix of the emerging craft of information design and six years of visual solution implementation success, and yet the mountain of businesses that have yet to engage suggests that this is the perfect time for the release of this book.

# REFERENCES

All of the images supplied in this book have been created by Frame Concepts. All the arguments are from the author and based purely on his 20 years of struggles with communication on the client side and visual solution successes on the Frame Concepts agency side of the house.

# ABOUT THE AUTHOR AND THIS BOOK

- First-Hand Knowledge of Communication Challenges and Visual Solution

- Presented from the Perspective of a Business Person, not a Designer

# FIRST-HAND KNOWLEDGE OF COMMUNICATION CHALLENGES AND VISUAL SOLUTIONS

While the author provides a lot of detail about the argument for visual solutions in business and insights into many applications with actual examples, the insights of the author are purely experience-driven through the actual experience of tackling business communication challenges. As the founder and CEO of a visual solutions agency based in New York—Frame Concepts—over the last five years, the author has front-line experience with hundreds of cases, not only in the oversight of the execution of the visual solutions but also in the pre-solution stage, talking to clients about the communication challenges they are suffering.

Moreover, as showcased in the second section of the book, these communication challenges have taken place within every major industry, business profession, and organization type: startups, enterprises, and non-profits. Most of the author's appreciation of clients' communication challenges have come from the 25 years before Frame Concepts on the client side, working as an engineering technologist in the early 80s, a training manager in a direct marketing agency in the 90s, and a host of tech startups in New York's "Silicon Valley" and marketing and communication roles at IBM and Wall Street. The author also has first-hand experience trying to communicate to undergraduate and graduate students on dense abstract topics within the discipline of philosophy at the University of Western Ontario and at City University of New York and on business and marketing topics at the Metropolitan College of New York.

# PRESENTED FROM THE PERSPECTIVE OF A BUSINESS PERSON, NOT A DESIGNER

This book is unique in that the author is not an information designer. He is literally the "client." In his 30 years of experience, he has both suffered from communication challenges in a marketing or communication leadership role, while now being at the vanguard of a comprehensive set of visually centric solutions leading Frame Concepts for the last five years. This is the book I wished I had read before my 30 years of trial and error tackling challenging business communication projects. In fact, until recently I think there has been an industry blind spot thinking that copy and traditional graphic design and branding is the best we can do to make our marketplace and our employees understand and engage with the point at hand. Based on his experience, this author has written this book to show we do not have to rest on this false assumption and to demonstrate through argument and example in order to convince and encourage the readers that the information design craft and visual solutions can solve THEIR business communication challenges.

# ABOUT THIS BOOK

Three Main Sections

# THREE MAIN SECTIONS

This book is divided into three main sections. The first section—Why Visual Solutions in Business?—talks about the argument for using visual solutions for business communications. The second section—Planning and Managing the Visual Solution Process in Your Business—speaks to planning and executing. The third section—Visual Solutions in Business Action—showcases visual solutions in action by providing a comprehensive portfolio, all in a business context. Why not just go right to application of visual solutions? Well, part of the "revolution" of using visual solutions for business communications is still partly, well . . . a revolution in progress. It has not been wholesale adopted by the marketplace. This is partly the reason for this book. There is an explicit suggestion that the author strongly believes that the reader should have already jumped onboard. The author is imagining

that the typical reader and his or her associates are, to varying degrees, still on the fence. Some are over the fence and convinced this is the way to make their content easy to understand and, perhaps more importantly, engage their audience with their content. Others are only halfway there: there are other competing interests, they are concerned that visuals may insult the intelligence of their audience, visuals may play havoc with their sophisticated brand, typical bandwidth and budget issues, and so on.

Again, this book introduces the reader to the "craft" of deploying visual solutions. Each chapter builds the argument and gives advice for deploying visual solutions.

**The first part** of the book is a wakeup call and sustained argument for organizations to use a visual solution approach. It is writ-

ten partly for people who must be convinced that visual solutions even have a place in business communications and also for employees who already are convinced, but need to bolster their argument to management and budget-keepers that the move makes sense.

**Part 2** assumes that the organization is moving forward with visual solutions and provides practical steps to successfully deploy them, including scoping the visual project, getting your team onboard, considering different visual supplier types, managing the creative process, and showing visual solutions. For those who already want to deploy visual solutions, this second section will show them practically how to plan and manage the process and the third section will show the myriad ways organizations—small and large—are deploying visual solutions to great effect.

**Part 3** is a visual tour de force
showcasing visual solutions of
every type of major industry, profession, and organization. For those
who are still not convinced, I hope
the third section showcasing how
their peers are leveraging visuals at
least causes organizations that may
be losing competitive advantage
to think about it, and that possibly
some lesser competitive player,
by leveraging visual solutions, will
bring part of their marketplace to an
understanding.

# INTRODUCTION: NOTES FROM THE UNDERGROUND

# MY CAREER LIFE IS SYMPTOMATIC OF OUR BUSINESS COMMUNICATION CHALLENGES

My whole academic and career life has been dotted with complex subject matter and the different approaches to get "the point" across. Of course, in the 30-plus years since graduating with a college diploma in mechanical engineering technology, I never really came to terms with the importance of communication until later in life. Now I see the pattern.

Like many of us, I felt it was something that one lives with and does the best he can with the tools and techniques available. But writing a book like this certainly puts one into a reflective spirit, and with the benefit of 20/20 hindsight, I can see the writing on the wall that modern visual solutions through the information design discipline was what was needed. In my defense, for the bulk of my career, they simply had not matured enough. Now they have.

Here is a brief synopsis of my back-ground that, I hope, will elicit a point of recognition with their communication struggles, and in full transparency, it is a bit of a defense that my background is a suitable melting pot for me to have the audacity to write such a book. For I am not an information designer or interactive or animation programmer, but instead I am the proverbial "client." I have seen the struggle and impact that not getting marketplace understanding and engagement produces, and I have seen hundreds of visual projects as the founder and CEO of a visual solution agency across many industries dealing with marketing and product and operations and technical teams for startups and large enterprises. Through my history here, I also hope to elicit a concern that the reader will identify with. Effective communication is hard with complex subject matter, and the business stakes are very high to get it right.

# MY FIRST BUSINESS COMMUNICATION LESSON: EXPLAINING THE BUSINESS VALUE OF PREVENTATIVE MAINTENANCE

Even in a non-communications role, stretching back to the early 1980s as a budding mechanical engineering technologist in a large petroleum plant, one of our key challenges with keeping rotating equipment running efficiently was to communicate to the process operators and mechanics and management the benefit of preventative maintenance programs. The costs to keep electric motors, compressors, turbines, pumps, fans, and diesel engine backups running was considerable, but the impact of failure was significant because of both repair costs and operational downtime and, in some cases, human safety. As a young college graduate and new employee, I was tasked with the rather administrative assignment of gathering maintenance record details and making recommendations on maintenance programs with a large report. I was out of my league. Managers ate me up when I presented, as they had more pressing concerns with losing millions of dollars a week when pump marketplace price pressures meant they were losing money every day of production. None of them could remember a significant failure on the equipment I spoke about. Perhaps one of the closing lines by a manager was the funniest and most symbolic: "I have a great idea. Why don't we shut down the plant so we don't lose any money on production and we won't need to spend any money on Mr. Gamble's preventative maintenance program. Kill two birds with one stone!" My sell of a preventative maintenance program failed miserably, and I had my first lesson: the importance of communications and a two-pronged theme that will color this book. I missed them on understanding and on engagement. And here I was not trying to sell a potential client—this was a part of our organization that supposedly had the same interests at heart.

# ACADEMIC COMPLEX COMMUNICATIONS

After a few years at engineering, I went to grad school and completed a master's degree in philosophy and did some doctorate work. Here, in terms of explaining complex and subtle concepts, I was pushed to the extreme. Everyday concepts like "truth," "reality," "good," and "meaning" were treated as exotic species of animals that needed to be studied. And different schools of thought or approaches like "realism" or "rationalism" or "linguistic idealism" would offer approaches to come to terms with understanding these cherished concepts and present merits and detriments compared to other schools of thought. I never have been challenged as much on the communication front to bring a young undergraduate fresh out of high school to the finer details of issues associated say with free will and determinism.

But one of these philosophical schools of thought that stayed with me in my business career was the notion of a conceptual framework—the idea that part of our cognitive apparatus imposes a conceptual net over experience and breathes in concepts to our understanding—became a formative part of my thinking. Most notably in the subject of Philosophy of Social Science, where modern Western anthropologists were coming to "primitive" societies like the Azande and wondering how objective their findings on their practices and beliefs are or whether in fact they were bringing their own Western notions into the analysis. Or put starkly, do we ever come to terms with reality outside the bounds of our human conceptual network?

While it may seem a stretch to bring such considerations into the business communications context, the toned down notion of simply coming to terms with your marketplace's frame of reference is important to how you position your offering and approach. You want them onboard, and so you have to bring them to a common point of reference. One of the key challenges is: When the organization really is offering innovation, how does one bring the point and value of such an approach that is operating in a more traditional framework with traditional toolsets? As you can imagine, I think Visual Solutions are key to shaking up the marketplace's framework and engaging them to one's innovative point of view.

# CORPORATE TRAINING

My jump post-philosophy graduate program into the business world was rather abrupt, but I was able to transition my academic teaching into corporate training at a marketing agency, which in turn brought me into the marketing craft in the mid-90s. And now, in the context of a marketing agency delivering on leads and conversion, time and revenue became paramount concerns. The agency was a bit of boilermaker. It was pre-Internet marketing—both aggressive outbound direct mail and telemarketing for large telcos and financial institutions and appointment setting for B2B services. The turnover rate was high, and the marketing contracts we owned were fragile, depending on the metrics we hit each month. My job was to come to terms with the corporate programs quickly and turn them around into a one-week training program that would bring mostly customer service reps into operational "performers" for the few months or even weeks we could keep them.

Reflecting back, 20 years later, I do remember that our client corporate managers who would from time to time check up on the quality of our services and come into my live training sessions were impressed mostly by scenario-centric training. Some of them noted the visuals I would sketch on the whiteboard to bring the trainees into some of the more technical aspects of the program were helpful. I would ask them to consider putting them into a training kit to make it easier to bring them onboard, but with razor-thin budgets, no one took me up on it. Such logic puzzled me, as the few years that I was there I literally must have trained thousands of reps, and reduced training time and absorption and retention rates would easily have paid for a few visual training aids. But yet another lesson: budgets tied to communications often seem a luxury item and not tied directly to the bottom line. And yet, marketplace and employee understanding and engagement with the business goals and offerings ARE tied to the bottom line. Defeating this logical tension has been a life-long challenge.

# WALL STREET

I was finally able to merge some of my technology background and comfort level with newly found communications and marketing prowess into one role. But instead of mechanical, the technical content was applications and hardware. When I was in high school, dating myself here, the computer science program was run on card readers. And in my first engineering role, there were no computers on anyone's desk. We all marveled when the secretary for our department at the end of the hallway from our offices had a new computer on her desk and could correct typing mistakes on the fly. While I saw merits and unsuccessfully argued to transfer our ink on cardboard maintenance records to start detecting patterns, I had no idea how computer science was going to catapult to the industry staple it has become.

Jump forward to late 90s and joining a top ten brokerage when trading applications and clearing services were all the rage. White labeling some of our applications and services to other brokerages become part of our go-to market plan, but we had to be able to communicate how they worked and the point of them to a trader or clearing department. So my communications went a bit technical using Microsoft Word and, for more robust operating guides, FrameMaker, and for online support, turning to RoboHelp and RoboHTML.

The client teams needed a sales tool to introduce the white-labeled offering to other trading partners, so we served up brochures with a bit of "style" with a long list of technical features the sales team could speak to. But it was a funny marketplace to market to. Our first customer segment was within our own company with departments with older applications, including our own lines of business on the trading and clearing floor. Once they found their way with our own staff and offered operating efficiencies, then we would turn to our partners. But in both cases, internal and external clients already had a solution—we needed to show that the new technology offered compelling value. A big move at that time was to build more flexible solutions with object-oriented programming. But our trader clients were always nervous about a new system. One day I went to the floor to one of the traders to ask him about the merits of a new system just being introduced so I could turn it into brochureware for external client business development. I did not know that it literally was being used the first time when I went onto the floor. The application had some hiccups and was causing

havoc with my trader contact, and he proceeded to throw equipment around and then openly berated the lead programmer in front of me and the rest of the floor. But as all our projects were funded by trading lines of business, we had to take the temperamental nature of our client in stride.

After a few years, a pattern or approach emerged to me to make the communication projects successful. It was steeply entrenched in unpacking communication layers. First there is the jargon of Wall Street, and then integrating the technology into a positioning statement that translated to value for nuanced need of the line of business. As none of them was technical, the technical feature translation to business value became a core communication commodity. Then as the web matured, the communication vehicles matured too

so that designing for print and the web and interactive became part of our essential tool kit. Reflecting on what we produced —again 20/20 hindsight—it was terrible stuff. It demanded the audience pore through dry technical features, and there were no engagement features at all. At best, it was factually correct and assumed they were onboard. We brought in external graphic designers and schooled ourselves on current graphics applications, but the effort in the end was only to jazz the materials up or at least make them look "professional." There was, in the end, no real explanatory or engagement power in what we were creating. But this was the norm in the late 90s.

# THE STARTUP
# LAUNDRY MACHINE

Much to the chagrin of my fellow communications professionals in the brokerage, I came enthralled in the late 90s with the tech startup movement and left the comforts of a top 10 brokerage firm and jumped into a communications role at my first startup. (The top 10 brokerage ended up being one of the more famous first casualties of the financial crisis and bailout period we went through a few years ago.)

I worked at an embarrassing (or impressive, depending on how you look at it) number of startups. All in all, I have worked for ten startups and three Fortune 500s, a mid-size marketing agency, and three academic institutions.

By far the greatest learning experience was going through the trials and tribulations of startups. To give a sense of breadth and complexity of offerings and related marketing content topics here is a brief list of the startup offerings:

1. An ecommerce software publishing vendor

2. A meta data platform for trading applications

3. A mobile trading and banking application

4. A web-based electronic bill presentment and payment platform

5. An enterprise application integrated knowledge management tool

6. A global IT procurement and lifecycle service platform

7. A Linux-based operating system

8. A cross-channel social ecommerce tool

9. A web-based recruiting search and posting tool

10. An information design visual solution agency (my current company I founded!)

This is not easy stuff to explain to potential customers. I now realized that getting the marketplace understanding and engagement was a necessity for startup survival.

# A LOT AT STAKE
# WITH STARTUPS

After the initial excitement and audacity of a new offering looking to replace the established well-heeled offerings and the pinball machines and beanie bags and dogs at work wear a bit thin, there is this thing about making it as a business. The fervor with founders and the early employees just don't seem to make a dent on the marketplace understanding. They don't care and don't know who you are. Even when you get a bit of press or a key C-level meeting, the indifference and lack of understanding of the true innovation of your offering can be shocking. Even the new round of hires seem to have a watered-down sense of the point of the offering. It was very difficult to explain to employees the benefits of say a Debian kernel in a new Linux operating system. Imagine trying to sell that to external clients already entrenched in the industry standard operating system. You may have some talent on your business development team and some level of VC funding to attack the market. But what do you attack with? What is the vision you are trying to establish? How can you effectively show the marketplace.

As a marketing lead for these offerings, I struggled. There was very tangible evidence of the struggle. My first startup, no thanks to me, was well timed with no early competition and went public with an IPO that we all celebrated on the office floor together. It seemed so easy. But after competition starting trickling in and investors' love affair with dot-coms started to wane in the late 90s, the stories were not so positive. I saw my share of office mates packing their belongings as funding and office cuts and company closures took place. I saw a founder blocked from returning from lunch to the office as ▸

he became the scapegoat for all the company's woes. I saw VCs throw money at a series of different CEOs and droves of well-heeled sales executives go through the mill without even denting the marketplace. I saw negativity build up around the water cooler as despair settled in that one would never see market-place engagement, even though the startup really, really, really offered unique valuable innovation.

I had one hiatus from startups in the midst of these ten, another Fortune 500, a global IT solutions provider where we hobbled together disparate solutions that were the different internal divisions or sourced through acquisition. The sophistication and breadth of the solutions like information lifecycle management or cross-border data privacy were a huge part of their differentiation in that they could draw from their newly acquired consulting arm or the software group or an IT services group or our hardware group. We had "Monday morning" status relationships with our large clients, so introduction of our offerings was not a challenge, unlike my startup experiences. But sorting our departmental offering to our clients into an integrated "solution" was a challenge. We aligned the sales team by simply making a joint sell of the depart-mental offerings as a necessary condition to receive commissions. Positioning an integrated solution with a new acquisition that only days ago was a competitor to the parent company was a communi-cation challenge, as was getting the client employee base onboard with, for example, a new three-year vendor management program they needed to learn and get excited about. The solutions were excellent, but the communication efforts to win clients and onboard employees for delivery were not visually robust at all. At one of our presentations, the CSO of a large global financial firm, after reviewing our materials and receiving presentations from our distinguished partners, simply stated: "I don't get what you guys do."

# SOME VISUAL LIGHT AT
# THE END OF THE TUNNEL

There were some bright lights on the communication front and, looking back, I can see how getting that core positioning and approach down in a single visual is key. In one startup we had a PowerPoint slide we called the "spaghetti" slide because it was a hot mess— all 80s neon colors using PowerPoint drawing tools. But it was the only slide that encapsulated our complex IT lifecycle ecosystem, including our delivery engine and our client and partner strategy. If we only had 5 minutes at a key meeting, we would pull out the spaghetti slide. We onboarded a graphic designer and did some overnights simply using stylish slides and graphic design to make a better presentation deck. But while it was stylish, it confused people more, and we always resorted to the ugly spaghetti slide. We designed a new website with a newly hired designer and, at an embarrassing Monday 8 a.m. meeting, the lead VC asked who came up with the new website because he had showed it to friends and family and they still couldn't understand what we did and what the VC had put millions into. I put up my hand that I was responsible for the site.

# A SKETCH HELPS BUSINESS

Another bright light was at electronic bill presentment and payment startup; like many of the startups, we did not have the solution built yet. We were looking for beta clients. The business development team were looking for a deck to present to beta prospects. I was using a creative agency to come up with a design for the interface for the product, and again we just applied graphic design to pretty things up, and the client team was, understandably, not happy. Then by accident a colleague of one of the staff—I think a magazine artist—listened to a description of our offering and drew the complex payor and payee relationship with our platform on a napkin, including currency translation, dispute resolution, and transparency. There was the innovation on one page! I quickly scanned it and put it in the deck, and the business development team ran with it. It became our spaghetti slide.

# NETTING IT ALL OUT

My goal in taking the reader though my career and communication challenges is to suggest in no uncertain terms that businesses struggle in helping their market-place and employees to understand and engage with their offerings and points of view. In a way, my career is symptomatic of the times. While this opinion is biased and only one person's experiences, the experiences cut through decades in a variety of industries and professions and organization types. I hope that the reader self-identifies with my experiences and is reminded of the challenge and the importance of getting business communications right. As we will see in the third section of this book, I currently also have more than five years leading an information design agency of enabling clients from a broad array of industries and professions and of varying sizes with engaging industry and function-contextualized visuals. There is a happy ending here. Part 2 of this book offers practical steps to realize that end.

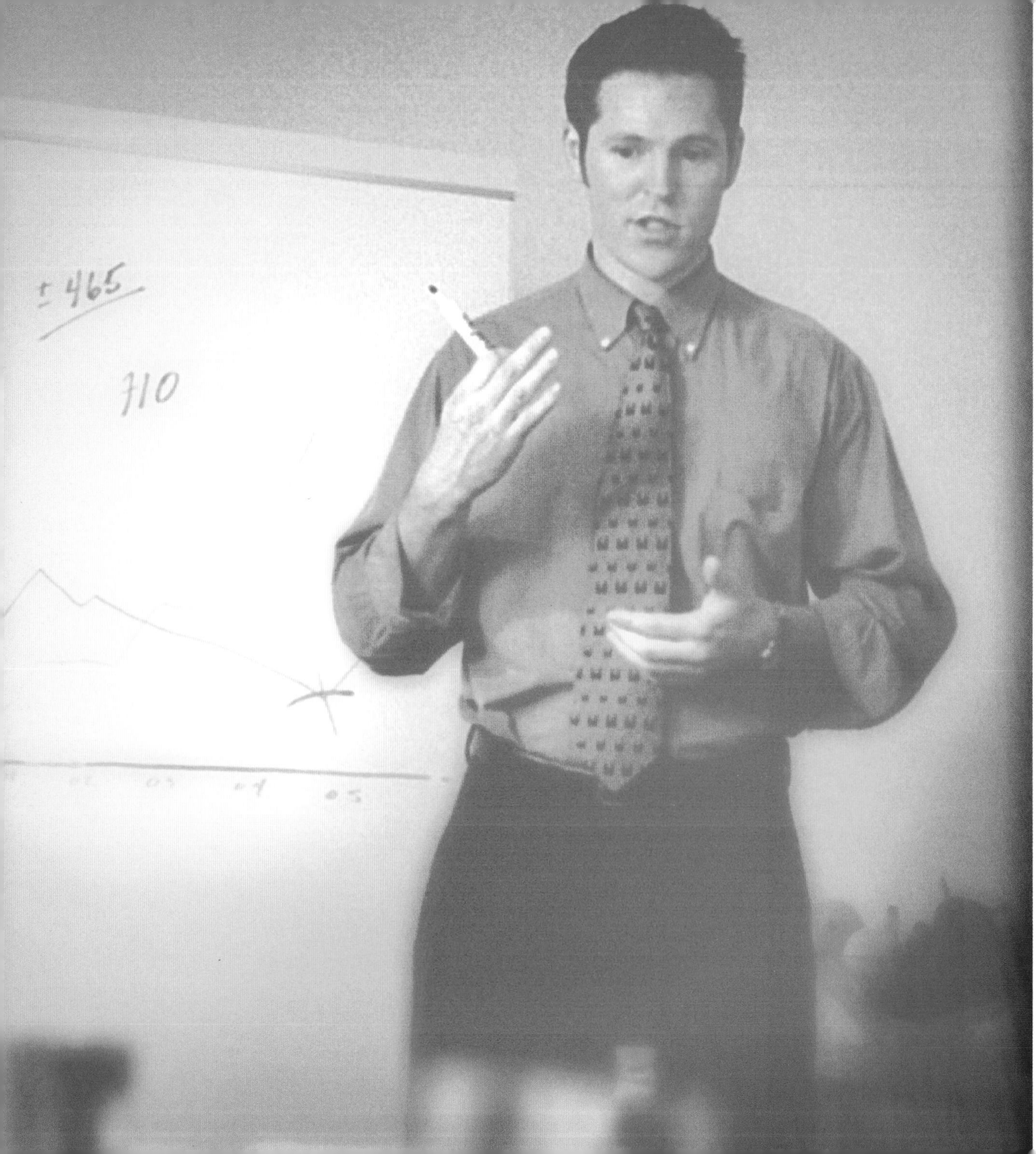
710

# PART 1

# WHY VISUAL SOLUTIONS FOR BUSINESS?

# WHY IS THERE A BUSINESS COMMUNICATION PROBLEM?

- Is Business Communication Important to the Bottom Line?
- So Why Is There a Communication Problem?
- Information Overload
- Information Economy
- Attention Deficit Syndrome
- Innovation Requires New Understanding
- Differentiation in a Crowded Space Very Nuanced
- Offerings Becoming Increasingly More Specialized
- Buyers Have No Time
- Media Consumption Increasingly Visual in the Media/Consumer World

# IS BUSINESS COMMUNICATION IMPORTANT TO THE BOTTOM LINE?

I suppose if one wanted to pull back to a high level and just talk about business communication writ large and its relevance when one is concerned about business success, I have come to the conclusion that if one cannot make the marketplace (and employees and management and partners) come to terms with what you are about—what you and your offerings are about—and you furthermore cannot motivate them to engage with your offerings, you have little chance of business success. Going back to the introduction and putting a bit of personal viewpoint into our analysis: all of the companies I worked for, especially the startups, were concerned about the marketplace "getting" them. They were concerned about the VCs; they were concerned about getting the right talent onboard and excited about the new vision; they were concerned about the beta clients;

they were concerned about the analysts and the media pundits; and of course they were concerned about the mainstream marketplace. From my experiences, it always felt like the company was on an inside track. They lived and breathed the new innovation—if only (and I repeat IF ONLY), the marketplace "got" them in the same way.

When I worked for a large IT consulting and services firm and we were pushing our new Security and Privacy practice that was integrating some of our new consulting acumen in the space with some of our new tech acquisitions, we presented to the chief security officer of a Tier 1 brokerage firm, a recent superstar hire from a large software vendor. He was VERY sharp. We flew in some of our top security talent, including a partner of the practice. The CSO was patient to a ▶

FrameConcepts

# Core to Business

## AUDIENCE UNDERSTANDING AND ENGAGEMENT KEY TO BUSINESS SUCCESS

www.frameconcepts.com

point during our capability presentation, and then he let us know what he really thought. He did not see that anything we were talking about had any value for his department. He asked a second time for us to explain what value we could offer to his firm. We did not satisfy him, and he suggested we come better prepared to communicate "relevance." At least he gave us another meeting.

This theme is a pattern, especially for complex offerings—a nuanced solution that speaks to a very intelligent audience, if only we could get them in the right mindset, in the right frame of reference, to appreciate our new point of view and new offerings and not let them lump us into a traditional offering category.

This is no joke. If you have seen divisions and companies close

and the impact it has, marketplace understanding and engagement is EVERYTHING. Of course, at the bottom, there has to be a differentiated offering that gives quantifiable value to its select marketplace. But once you have that and you have invested in the offering and the company's delivery capabilities, there is still just as big an issue (sometimes even bigger than product development itself): getting the marketplace onboard. And that does not happen unless they understand your offering and are motivated to engage. You have to capture their minds and their will and their hearts.

# SO WHY IS THERE A COMMUNICATION PROBLEM?

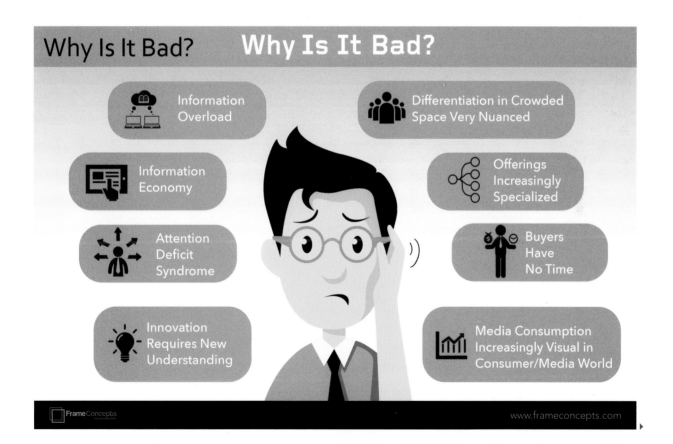

We will not spend too much time on this question for fear that most of us are on the practical side and want to get visual solutions in motion. For some of us, lack of marketplace understanding and engagement can be felt in one's business life every day, and we want not so much to appreciate why but learn how to solve the problem. But again, for our readers who are onboard the visual solution train and want to steer their organizations (and their budgets) toward a visually centric approach, they may want to appear reasonable; and that this is a problem that is everywhere in today's marketplace. The most conscious CFOs want to get the marketplace onboard and have clients writing checks for services as quickly and efficiently as possible, so they want the client to appreciate the offerings so they keep renewing, right?

If this is the immediate and end goal, it is best to take a look at the hard realities of the marketplace to see it is not easy and to come back with an approach (a visual approach, of course) to meet this problem head on.

There are lots of reasons why it is difficult to enable understanding and engagement in today's marketplace. A slide from one of our webinar presentations provides some key reasons. I do not think there is anything controversial here, and one could provide stats to back them up but, again, I think we just need to remind ourselves that this is the mountain we are trying to climb. We are clamoring for marketplace attention and, of course, understanding and engagement as we drive through our content funnel starting with raw awareness, to consideration, to evaluation, and to final negotiation.

Let's quickly remind ourselves what we are up against and perhaps tuck in some suggestions with how we are going to deal with the issues, at least at a high level. You can see detailed examples in the third part of this book and how to execute in the second part.

# INFORMATION OVERLOAD

The increase in specialized programs in colleges does not stop post-graduation. The average businessperson is faced with a myriad of typical learning curves. The marketing person in a technology company, for example, has to come to speed with the technology itself and think of how technical features translate to business value and then come up with positioning and creative ideas on how to get the point across. There are technical aspects to message delivery: social media, blogging, SEO, SEM, retargeting, email, and marketing automation and A/B testing of landing pages, trade shows and special events, white papers and client case studies, product road maps—and the list goes on. If the organization is targeting specific professions or industries, then the marketing person has to come to terms with their jargon, how they cut up the world, pain points, and relevant points of entry when communicating the new offering. Most professions are in a similar, layered learning curve juggling act.

Then, with your communications outreach program, you want to add to the pile they need to come to terms with. Let me tell you one thing not to do. Do not throw at them a twenty-page technical document with content and a stock photo of two executives jumping up for joy on the cover. Why not make it easy and, with one crisp visual, bring the readers' eyes and minds in and cleverly situate them and their business challenges within that visual and THEN bring your offering into the visual to show how it solves the issue and delivers that value.

# INFORMATION ECONOMY

As we move to a more information-based economy, surprise, surprise, the offerings are very information-based. That compounds the information overload problem as more competitive offerings are struggling to get their own information-based offerings to the marketplace. As we shall see in Chapter 2, information design is the perfect tool for the information economy. But everyone else's information and solution are running through the same information-based economy, and one needs to cut visually through the clutter.

# ATTENTION DEFICIT SYNDROME

This is more perhaps a symptom of our audiences suffering from information overload. But it's a catchy, perhaps over-used term to remind us that those moments you get a marketplace member to even consider your offering are few and far between. Those eyes are scanning over meeting notes, emails, websites, presentations and reports every day. Yet you want to put your communication about your offering under their noses. Again, a piercing visual—even a static print piece or an interactive or animated communication—CAN grab attention while at the same time carefully bring people to a state of understanding and engagement. The simplicity of the visual can convince the viewer that it will only take a moment to learn the point at hand.

# INNOVATION REQUIRES
# NEW UNDERSTANDING

The whole point to innovating is to disrupt the marketplace with something it does not have and sometimes ask others to approach the problem in a different way. You need people to come to a new frame of reference—YOUR frame of reference. You need to provoke. You don't want them to lump your approach and your offering into a traditional category. Visuals can carry the reader along. By simply visually scattering disparate traditional solutions across the world—all visually onto one circle, one platform—you are making an arresting statement suggesting you can reduce the complexity to one simple platform, making a huge operational impact on the original options. All with one visual. A secondary point: a carefully made visual communication piece signals to the audience that your company has put a lot of thought into the solution and enabling them to learn it, which causes them to care and to engage. The craft of the visual underscores the importance of the offering.

# DIFFERENTIATION IN A CROWDED SPACE VERY NUANCED

It's very rare today to introduce an offering that has no alternatives. Your client is typically carrying on a particular business activity already, but your approach suggests bold improvements. Certain benefits are only available through your offering. And perhaps you have already approached the analysts and the media to showcase this fact. But the analysts already are familiar with a dozen or so offerings that are "similar" to yours but are keen to see how yours is different. So you present to them as you would to your clients. They are probably going to see ten other presentations like yours. You need to stand out. When you present face-to-face or web share on a conference call, you need a visual that gets them quickly to your point or you will lose them.

# OFFERINGS BECOMING INCREASINGLY MORE SPECIALIZED

I did channel marketing for a software operating system. Their important differentiation was a Debian kernel for a Linux-based operating system. These fine points were differentiators in a specialized space as generations upon generations of offerings come onto market. But with the flexibility of a visual solution—starting with the complete flexibility of a pencil sketch—you can zero in on that particular aspect and surface the fine detail. You can zoom in or out like a virtual camera as it were, to any degree of detail that is necessary to tease out the positioning needed.

# BUYERS HAVE
# NO TIME

⎯⎯⎯⎯

Our marketplace has their "day jobs." We want to disrupt those day jobs for some precious moments so they can produce more value with our offerings. So if they have limited time, why would one (as is prevalent in today's communication channels) force people to go through pages and pages of a website filled with text and the occasional stock photo or scroll down endlessly to a series of text-only blogs, or even worse, on a product page you present a list of technical features with an occasional screenshot of the offering. Why not visually engage people with an easily digestible image that puts them into your offering so they can see the value quickly, understand the offering, and come to you with questions about their unique needs.

# MEDIA CONSUMPTION INCREASINGLY VISUAL IN THE MEDIA/CONSUMER WORLD

The media and consumer communication channels are not making things easier. Social channels—at least the ones that work and have impact—are becoming increasingly viral. Magazines and newspapers in both print and web formats are becoming increasing visual. One is shown step-by-step with a full-page infographic on how speculation with mortgage-based securities brought Wall Street to its knees a few years ago. *The New York Times,* Bloomberg, and others have infographic and data visualizations departments to engage readers with technical topics full of data points. Video is key to YouTube, but is also making its way to other social channels and blogs. We are living in a visual world. So your business communication has to compete. Why not join the visual world? The visual train has left the station, and you have to compete for your marketplace's attention with the same visual craft to enable understanding

AS MENTIONED EARLIER, THIS BOOK IS NOT INTENDED FOR A BUDDING INFORMATION DESIGNER, BUT MORE FOR BUSINESS PEOPLE WHO WANT (AFTER THEY ARE CONVINCED THEY SHOULD) TO DEPLOY VISUAL SOLUTIONS TO MEET BUSINESS GOALS. BUT IT MAY BE USEFUL TO CONTRAST THE CRAFT OF INFORMATION DESIGN WITH SOME OF THE OTHER CREATIVE DISCIPLINES TO SHOW WHAT THE BUSINESS PERSON IS UP AGAINST. THE READER, OR MORE LIKELY THE READER'S MANAGEMENT TEAM, MAY COUNTER THAT THEY HAVE TRIED VISUAL SOLUTIONS WITH TRADITIONAL GRAPHIC DESIGN AND SO WE NEED TO EXPLAIN THAT INFORMATION DESIGN IS DIFFERENT FROM THE USUAL SUSPECTS. INDEED, INFORMATION DESIGN, AS WE SHALL SEE, IS VERY DIFFERENT.

# SOLUTION: INFORMATION DESIGN

# GRAPHIC DESIGN VS. INFORMATION DESIGN

Most of us in the business communication fields have some graphic design chops or have leveraged the craft for communication projects. The graphic designer is typically challenged to come up with a layout in a pre-designated format leveraging static copy and images against a client's pre-approved branding guidelines or come up with those branding guidelines organically. The information designer does not take the data and the tables and the content as a pre-existing static unit cast in stone, but thinks about how to structure it in terms of hierarchies and display it and possibly replace or supplement data and charts with visuals. Perhaps a dense concept might be unpacked with a new infographic.

In earlier years, I personally went through the growing pains of trying to leverage graphic design resources to come up with an infographic type visual for a solution offering before the term "infographics" became popular. My graphic design resources were challenged on a few different fronts, and it became a pattern for me. First, they were not illustrators, so they were not going to pencil sketch a new conceptual visual to steer the piece, nor were they comfortable with lots of data and a hierarchy of content and thinking about how to unpack it to yield insight. They wanted a blueprint to guide them for both content and the visual. This new method was not core to what a graphic designer does.

# ILLUSTRATION VS. INFORMATION DESIGN

I have used former magazine illustrators also. They, of course, could illustrate. They create beautiful title page illustrations and spot illustrations, typically at the head of an article, to pull the reader into the content. And if there was a complete scoped-out visual instruction for a business communication project—perhaps a pencil sketch and all the salient callout boxes and labels and a style guideline—basically a visual blueprint instruction guide, I could get what I wanted from an illustrator. But with each new client we are faced with at our information design agency, of course no such visual blueprint instruction existed. That's why the client had come to us. The clients wanted us to unpack them, as they had tried and failed. Coming up with the salient core visual sketch that captures the ah-hah moment from clunky reference materials and a client debriefing is the hardest part. This is not the world of a typical illustrator, and most will be in over their heads as they become lost in the clients' jargon and are intimidated by the dense subject matter and challenged for how they are going to surface even an initial sketch that captures the essence of the point. Sometimes, it's not even a pure illustration that is needed, but it could be data visualization or a rearrangement of a form or table that is necessary.

# TECHNICAL COMMUNICATION VS. INFORMATION DESIGN

Now technical communicators—I have experience with this craft—do have a comfort level dealing with complex subject matter. They typically turn to programmers and product teams and unpack an offering into intuitive procedural manuals. Now if one were to pore through the operating manual, one could understand the product and how it works. But technical communicators have a much deeper problem in that they are trying to win the marketplace over to the solution at hand. For a lot of the reasons we listed in the previous chapter, like "information overload" and "attention deficit disorder," we can rarely get anyone to stay on a web page for more than 2 seconds, let alone pore through an operating manual. It just is not part of the technical communication craft that they be charged with visually engaging an online marketplace to consider their offerings. By the time they step in, that job is done, and they need to help the users become operational. But the point of this book is that the audience has to be engaged first.

# COPYWRITING AND STOCK PHOTO SOURCING

---

The copywriter can, however, think about how to position the offering with words and to make the content more visually interesting by sourcing photos and clip art (of course the graphic designer could do the sourcing also). Unfortunately, I have too much experience with this from the client side, and it really did not do a lot of good for engaging and explaining the point. The two together—copy with a photo at the top or placed somewhere in the piece—has now become the poster child of bad design. Almost all of my clients have this problem when they come to me. Of course, this can be a fruitful starting point for the visual craft discussion. We can see what our client is striving for by reading the copy and looking at the visuals, and then we can start the pencil sketching process to put it all in one, easy-to-digest, cohesive visual.

# SO HOW IS INFORMATION DESIGN DIFFERENT?

---

There are lots of "definitions" of information design. Again, the purpose here is not to train information designers or to learn how to do information design, but to learn how to leverage the craft for business purposes. Given all the concerns that have to be overcome to communicate a message, some important aspects of information design are more important from the perspective of a business manager. These aspects can counter concerns and offer what traditional graphic design, copywriting, and stock images cannot offer.

# THE INGREDIENTS OF INFORMATION DESIGN

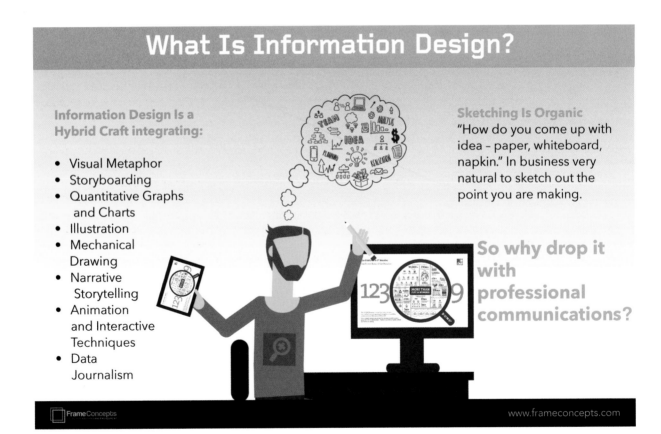

## What Is Information Design?

**Information Design Is a Hybrid Craft integrating:**

- Visual Metaphor
- Storyboarding
- Quantitative Graphs and Charts
- Illustration
- Mechanical Drawing
- Narrative Storytelling
- Animation and Interactive Techniques
- Data Journalism

**Sketching Is Organic**
"How do you come up with idea – paper, whiteboard, napkin." In business very natural to sketch out the point you are making.

**So why drop it with professional communications?**

FrameConcepts

www.frameconcepts.com

While it seems easy to sum up what information design is with its typical output types—illustration, icons, charts, typography, forms, and tables—on a certain level this misses the point or some of the benefits. It's helpful in that it contrasts information design with traditional graphic design because it illustrates new concepts, rather than just laying out and designing pre-existing content.

There is a performance component to any information design project. How can we take all the data and content, find the real point, and come up with a communication piece that is easy to understand and that engages the audience? The information designer has to find the point being made and the underlying argument or narrative BEFORE beginning any visual work. While this is most true for marketing tools and websites and training, even for data-driven visualizations and applications, the information designer has to think through the relevant user profiles and workflow and business goals before visually designing the best interface.

For the business person, this is all good. You want the information designer on your side of the communication struggle—with all the compelling features and benefits or insightful points of view suited for a variety of audience segments. How should the designer approach the point visually? This is squarely your business problem, and you now have the right craft to solve the problem. The solution is not to fill a presentation, brochure, or website with loads of content and a few stock photos. Rather, effective information design comes with a very important tool to help ideate a visual solution—a pencil.

# PENCIL SKETCH: DRIVING VISUAL IDEATION

We will go into the process and management of the entire "create" process in a later chapter, but it is hard for me to think about information design without a pencil sketch. While developing a polished rendering and using sophisticated interactive and animation programming techniques to bring the visual project to life certainly has impact, it's in the early stages—the pencil sketch ideation phase—that the designer learns the power of information design.

In what seems like a simple output—a pencil sketch—there is a lot going on beneath the surface. First, there is typically a metaphor or analogy or narrative theme in play. Dense content is being unpacked by a simple visual. There should be enough detail in the sketch that one has that "ah-hah" moment where the point immediately strikes the reader and engages him or her.

Tough decisions are made about what to keep and what to take out of the client's reference materials and debriefing are suggested through the sketch. Typically something that's a bit technical is now presented in terms more digestible by the viewer. Not bad for a simple sketch.

This is how it goes for me in my role when leading complex visual solution efforts. As the years go by and the projects total in the hundreds, I am always, as are the clients, impressed by the robustness at play with the information design craft. This robustness and creativity and ability to go from blank page to tangible visual ideation is the cornerstone of information design and why it's both different from traditional graphic design and well-suited for business communications. Each business has nuance solutions with a very

particular vision for its end-user. With information design—starting with a pencil sketch—a visual concept can be created that meshes with the solution the client presents and fits within the audience's framework. One had infinite flexibility with a pencil, a blank page, and the craft of information design.

WE ARE STARTING TO SEE WHY THE CRAFT OF INFORMATION DESIGN MAKES SUCH A GOOD SOLUTION FOR OUR BUSINESS COMMUNICATION CONCERNS ABOUT AUDIENCE UNDERSTANDING AND ENABLEMENT. THERE ARE OTHER SYNERGIES THAT MAKE THIS CRAFT EVEN MORE COMPELLING.

# LEVERAGING INFORMATION DESIGN FOR BUSINESS COMMUNICATIONS: A PERFECT STORM

- The Audience Already Enjoys Visual Communication in Media and Consumer Channels

- The Rise of Content and Inbound Marketing

- Data Analytics Has Become Mainstream

- Value and Solution Selling Have Become the Norm

# THE AUDIENCE ALREADY ENJOYS VISUAL COMMUNICATION IN MEDIA AND CONSUMER CHANNELS

First, for a few years now the infographic has been a staple for explaining more complex ideas for publications such as *Fast Company, USA Today, The New York Times,* and *The Wall Street Journal.* The craft of information design has matured through use in divisions of the media houses, and we have become accustomed as vast consumers of complex topics to allow an infographic to take us through a complex narrative. It's quick. It's easy. It's sharable. And it's fun. And now businesses can leverage the craft for their unique business communication goals.

# THE RISE OF CONTENT AND INBOUND MARKETING

Second, for the past few years, content or inbound marketing has become all the rage for engaging a business audience. Instead of blitzing one-way outbound emails on promotional offers and disguised sales sheets, we have learned to offer rewarding content relevant to our audience's business goals and professional development that also subtly brings in the client's point of view or unique offering. Marketing automation in mature organizations enables the marketing department to nurture their audience base with workflow-triggered and relevant content based on the audience's reactions to previous content. The emphasis is on coming up with engaging content to feed the content marketing engine. Again, a perfect storm for leveraging visual solutions crafted with information design principles.

# DATA ANALYTICS HAS BECOME MAINSTREAM

Finally, analytics for the past years has become the business superstar with people with titles like "data scientist" finding their way onto management teams, along with the traditional operations, sales and marketing, technology, finance, and administration titles. Indeed, in addition to cloud-based offerings, organizations boasting analytics tools and capabilities have become a major client type for us at Frame Concepts.

In terms of business communications performance, its commonplace to run analytics on web pages to learn about visitor traction and/or abandonment. While the landing page and perhaps the home page receive most of the attention, when we take dry text and a stock-image-based product or solution page and enable it with interactive visual solutions—like an interactive solution pictogram—we can certainly move the needle in terms of visitor engagement, which has a direct correlation with audience understanding and engagement. Just as we have turned the corner with content programs to advance marketplace awareness and consideration by leveraging infographics, we can also think about improving conversion rates with a call to action for web-based visual communications.

# VALUE AND SOLUTION SELLING HAVE BECOME THE NORM

Instead of delineating a host of technical features, enlightened marketing and sales programs now show how the offering delivers value and solves the client's business problems. The key now is not to tell them about your impressive product features, but instead show them how to achieve their business goals with your differentiated solution. As we have seen, visuals are king for quickly engaging the audience in using your solution for solving their problems. Visuals simply show the differentiated value better than traditional product feature lists do.

# THE ARGUMENT FOR VISUAL-CENTRIC APPROACH

# WHY ARE VISUAL SOLUTIONS SO EFFECTIVE IN BUSINESS COMMUNICATIONS?

The robustness of the information design craft and its ability to ideate almost anything on a blank page representing a client's point of view or offering is a perfect marriage. With content marketing concerns around awareness and engagement and analytic concerns around conversion, information design is a perfect vehicle to deliver and test the effectiveness of sophisticated custom visuals.

All the concerns we raised about the different understanding and engagement issues are met with information design. Information overload and attention deficit disorder and a client's typically short available time to consider anything are addressed with a compelling single visual. And nuanced, specialized offerings captured in engaging visuals can break audience preconceptions. Because the visuals are so simple, prospects quickly realize the point at hand and are motivated to engage with the visual communication. This is the general idea for why to use visual solutions in business communications. Here are a few further arguments in case you need to bring your team and/or management onboard.

# VISUALS IN BUSINESS: THE PSYCHOLOGICAL ARGUMENT

This is easy. Just do a Google search on visuals increasing learning and retention, and you will find no shortage of research results. Here is one such sample:

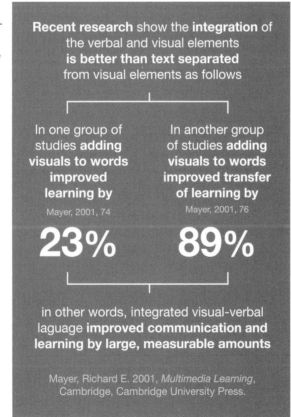

**Recent research** show the **integration** of the verbal and visual elements **is better than text separated** from visual elements as follows

In one group of studies **adding visuals to words improved learning by**
Mayer, 2001, 74

**23%**

In another group of studies **adding visuals to words improved transfer of learning by**
Mayer, 2001, 76

**89%**

in other words, integrated visual-verbal laguage **improved communication and learning by large, measurable amounts**

Mayer, Richard E. 2001, *Multimedia Learning*, Cambridge, Cambridge University Press.

Not really a bold claim. Also keep in mind that interactive projects help with engagement. Of course, with video one has both the audible words and in some cases music to add to the learning and retention benefits.

# VISUAL SOLUTIONS IN BUSINESS: THE MARKETING METRIC ARGUMENT

These psychological benefits translate to business benefits in terms of higher sales. Again, a quick Google search on email, social media, or blog benefits with visuals produces a myriad of data indicating better business results. Here is one such list compiled from one of our webinar presentations:

 **In**

**People love infographics and the stats back it up**

Color Visuals increase the willingness to read by

80%

 **Improves Ease Understanding**

Adding Visuals to Words Improved Transfer of Learning by

80%

 FrameConcepts
VISUAL EXPLANATIONS AND ENGAGEMENT

# ormation Design Works

 **Retain It Longer**

Recall

**80%**
of what
you SEE

**20%**
of what
you READ

 **Get It Quicker**

One can understand a VISUAL scene
in less than one-tenth of a second
because visuals are processed
**60,000** times faster in the brain.

Infographics are "liked" 4X
more than presentations
and 23X more than
documents on SlideShare.

www.frameconcepts.com

# VISUAL SOLUTIONS IN BUSINESS: THE ORGANIC ARGUMENT

This is less of an argument and more a logical extension of what we said above. It strikes me as very natural or "organic" when trying to convey a point to a colleague in a business setting to go to a whiteboard and sketch the concept out. Or within product teams, while they are ideating on direction or strategic partnerships, it's also natural to sketch out different options on a whiteboard. Or for a startup to use a whiteboard to ideate new ideas. Or for a corporation offsite meeting to break into work groups and use markers and poster paper to capture some of the ideas from the group to take back to the rest of the team. Indeed, it's the start of the conversation. Then the other group members go to the whiteboard to edit or simply gesture to different parts of the sketch to make their points.

When we present to a prospect or at an event, we use slides to speak to something visual. When we teach, we use a blackboard with chalk. If we are at lunch, we might simply draw on a napkin. It's for a good reason: because you want your colleagues or your audience onboard with your point. You want to bring others to your understanding, your frame of reference, your point of view. You want to reference something to advance the communication and hear others' input. You want others referring to the same visual.

So when we want to take an offering to market, why would that natural instinct stop? Why wouldn't we want a professional information design to get it just right? Your prospect has not been exposed to all the sketches on the whiteboard that your team debated and refined.

These arguments and sketches got your team and management onboard. Don't you want those who are going to pay for your services to visualize your solution? If it was so natural to ideate over sketches to make your point internally, why wouldn't it be extended to your prospects, leveraging the latest information design features?

# OPPOSING THE FINANCIAL (OR LUXURY) ARGUMENT

Well perhaps you are convinced at this point, and hopefully you have convinced your management team armed with budget to start your visual programs. But there is one remaining argument we should consider before we go the Second Part of the book and put visuals into action. So the opposing point of view could argue—"well I see that having our key communication interfaces— corporate presentations, websites, product brochures, social sites etc.—could benefit from the craft of information design. But I have seen infographics and animations and these visual solutions before and they really are the 'luxury' of media outlets and consumer entertainment fields. We are a business—we are not here to get magazine or newspaper subscription rates up nor are we here to entertain children on Saturday morning television programs. We are not going to turn to 'cartoons' to help our bottomline."

I have a bit of thin skin with this argument as I have suffered from it both on the client and agency side. It is hard to generically quantify the ROI of a visual solution across industries and so I typically turn to a logical consistency-based argument. I remind my audience how much they have invested in the solution—including producing the product or solution, staffing the organization, importance of first to market and getting whole marketplace adoption, and the unusual innovation of the solution itself. At the bottom of each of these points there is a tremendous confidence in the client that they have the differentiated solution that will drive their marketplace's business goals that no one else has and they know they have to convince the marketplace and influencers of this fact. So if so much time, money, staff, effort, emotional energy with time to market pressures in play, from a consistency point—why would you stop short and not try to visually convey this point in the most intuitive and engaging way possible. The cost of information design seems miniscule compared to the typical investment and the cost of not getting marketplace understanding and engagement as quickly as possible is in my view professionally negligent. And as we shall see in the coming chapters—the competition is starting to get onboard the visual solution train. There is no excuse (or argument) not to engage.

# PART 2

# PLANNING AND MANAGING THE VISUAL SOLUTION PROCESS IN YOUR BUSINESS

# STRATEGY – SCOPING IN VISUAL SOLUTIONS TO YOUR ORGANIZATION

# WHERE TO START?

---

Well, now that we have seen the argument for visual solutions in business communication, we turn to getting onboard and planning the visual solution itself. The range of business applications that one can apply visual solutions to—as shown in Part 3—is both intriguing and daunting at the same time. Where to begin? Quite often clients at our information design agency come to us with a particular project or topic or offering that they need help with. But sometimes the initial conversation is more wide-ranging, and the client is curious where one can apply these types of solutions. And the easy answer is everywhere.

But we have to start somewhere and need a plan for scoping them in. Let's look at some considerations.

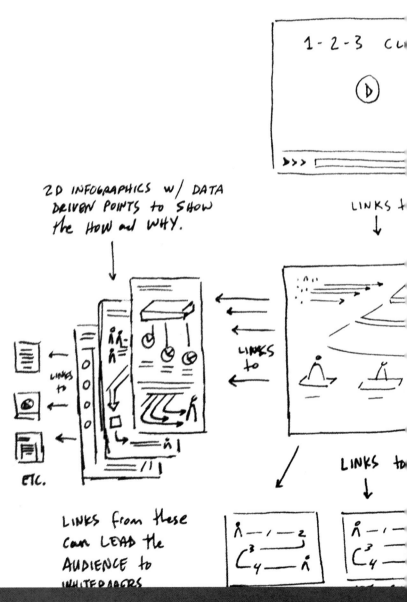

VISUAL NETWORK SYSTEMS CAMPAIGN APPROACH:

THIS COULD BE DESIGNED to LIVE ON BOTH a WEBSITE OR INTERACTIVE PDF that could BE EMAILED or DOWNLOADED.

1-2-3 CL

2D INFOGRAPHICS w/ DATA DRIVEN POINTS to SHOW the HOW and WHY.

LINKS t

LINKS to

LINKS to

ETC.

LINKS from these can LEAD the AUDIENCE to WHITEPAPERS

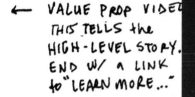

← VALUE PROP VIDE[O]
THIS TELLS the
HIGH-LEVEL STORY.
END W/ A LINK
to "LEARN MORE..."

← OVERVIEW / ECOS[YSTEM]
INTERACTIVE PICT[URE]

LINKS FROM H[ERE]
MOVE THROUGH
FOR BOTH AUDI[ENCE]
TYPES and TE[CH]
"HOWs and WH[YS]
DATA SPEC[I]

◄ *A typical*
*scoping sketch*

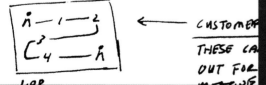

← CUSTOME[R]

THESE CA[N]
OUT FOR
[MA]TU[RE]

# CONSIDERATIONS

————

Of course, the budget is a consideration. It can help inform how wide and deep one can go. We typically take a client though pricing for varying solutions after we have a sense of the context and need. Given they are still considered by some as "progressive," "out on the frontier," "unusual," or however one may put it, the client may want to take baby steps and show value to the rest of his or her organization, especially to management.

So although it is highly context-based—almost like the creative visual solutions themselves—if the client asks for my advice on how to start, I typically talk about scope and strategy with visual solutions, what better way than with a visual scoping sketch!

# IT ALL STARTS AT HOME

Even if the client's goal is leads and awareness, I suggest that the client first make sure the offering and their point of view—their positioning—is presented visually. Invariably, no matter how effective and "thick" a visual, integrated lead management program is, the prospect will come to your site to receive a presentation of your offering and your value proposition. That communication better be as intuitive and engaging visually as possible to drive the prospect to do business with you; otherwise, you're wasting your lead program investment and driving them to your website and your sales team presentation that does not convert effectively.

Look at the sample scoping sketch above. I suggest that you come to terms with the value proposition of your company at a high level with an animated infographic video.

In about 200 words or 60 to 90 seconds, we help the viewer on your website or YouTube channel or trade show or banner ad or even in a link from your sales team to see that you have a differentiated value proposition that speaks to their pressing business need. Of course, that just gets you into their awareness and the consideration stage of your marketing funnel. From there, we suggest the prospect go to the interactive solution pictogram—typically on the solution or services section of your website and possibly embedded in your sales presentation and trade show screen displays. Here they dive more deeply and interact with your solution at a high business level, learning more about the differentiated features of your solution now they realize from looking at the video that your company approaches the marketplace in a unique and intriguing way. While the interactive pictogram is a deeper dive than the animated infographic video, it is not a technical manual or technical data sheet. It is still speaking to three to five benefits to a select audience that includes buyers, influencers, and gate-keepers.

The bonus from visually positioning your company and its offerings is that, quite often, the experience of creating visual solutions drives ideas for the content programs that are yet to come. We find it's a good idea to take notes on some of these ideas, as it's common to realize that content that's too much to tackle in one pictogram or animation could be perfect for an infographic to feed the content marketing engine. The animation and the pictogram typically serve as the theme—the battle plan—for the content of the outreach program. Knowing the prospect will be funneled to these visual explanations helps shape the narrative of each infographic and keeps your content team focused as they develop the editorial calendar. Again, a lot of good ideas will flow out of the debates and hard editorial discussions you have as you create your core visual explanations around your company and your offerings, so I repeat: take careful notes!

Looking back at the scoping sketch above, we have a value proposition animation in place and an interactive solution pictogram for the offering(s). These will help, especially in your website on the conversion front. It's difficult not to click on a play button or an interactive image on a provocative visual that speaks on a topic that is your pressing business concern. One may not have time for a full sales presentation or even to read a white paper, but one can squeeze in 60 seconds for a fun, information animation or click through an interactive solution pictogram that is speaking to one's business problem in a unique and provocative way. Neither of these solutions is designed to close the sale, but they should engage viewers and aid their understanding enough for them to want to learn more from your sales team and hit the relevant call to action—a free demo or consultation, or whatever the case might be.

# ON TO CONTENT MARKETING

---

Of course, no one ever achieves 100 percent conversion and you have to get the prospect to your website to begin with. In 2016, content marketing is all the rage, and we are learning not to drive the marketplace away with "salesy" one-way communication blasts. Instead, we are adapting an enlightened inbound content marketing program where we cleverly come up with content that educates, inspires, amuses, and engages our target audience with information they want to consume, but also weaves in client offerings or unique points of view. But as clever as we are with this weaving, it's challenging to try to engage with traditional content—pages of textual and data content—even in the most stylish blog, newsletter, or paper format. This is where the mighty infographic is king.

Of all the visual solutions we speak to in this book, the infographic seems to be the most well-known and "hot" for marketing purposes. The client is sometimes surprised that I use them as an extension of the more product marketing–oriented visual solutions—the interactive solution pictogram and the value proposition animation.

# VALIDATING YOUR APPROACH AND YOUR SOLUTIONS

Looking again at the scoping sketch, on the third row down, labeled "Customer Stories" on the right, we see another integrated layer of communications. Here I am making more of a marketing suggestion: now that we have showcased value in the form of animations and an interactive solution pictogram and brought the client into the conceptual fold—given them a frame of reference with the extended infographic series—now I am concerned about whether their marketplace will accept the logic and merits of the solution after being engaged with these visual solutions. Experienced business buyers have seen solutions that on paper logically made sense only to find that something is awry.

At this point, we want empirical data—preferably actual clients who have used the solution—to confirm the promised value does actually get delivered in the trenches. We want this quantified. But even armed with such data, how do we get the prospect to engage with the communication of it. Surprise, surprise, we advocate visuals to the rescue once again. But this time we turn to classic data visualization to present in an intuitive and action-inspiring fashion. This presentation could take the form of case studies, presentation slides, reports, or if it's something the client wants to express continually against a moving database, it could be a data-driven visualization in a web browser or application.

# SALES TOOLS

Looking again at our scoping sketch, we turn to the bottom row, which we can refer to as sales tools. Here we want to take the client's complete story—their core positioning—that we arrived at with the corporate value proposition animation, the interactive solution pictogram, the editorialized colored points of view, and best practices contained in the infographic series and the data-driven customer success stories. We want to arm the entire organization—especially the sales team—with the same compelling visual tools. So we take the vector art from the original visual solutions and reformat them to presentations, brochures, papers, and signage.

# GETTING EVERYONE ONBOARD

It helps if you are working with an experienced information design firm, as they can provide live demos, samples of sketches, polished visuals, and discussion of approaches to soften those in your team who think you have gone off the deep end with cartoons! At Frame Concepts, we take our clients through a representative of relevant visual samples based on client needs. Quite often a few samples leap to the front of the conversation and are useful catalyst to help create the visual solution that is most relevant for that client. Of course, as these visual solutions are new to our marketplace, some of the samples showcase capabilities that they did not know were possible and, then "need" becomes very fluid as they realize they can accomplish business communication goals in ways they did not think were possible.

But once a scope is settled on and a delivery plan is formed (see Chapter 7 on Managing Vendors: A Repeatable Creative Process), it's important that the entire organization embrace the new visual-centric approach. Perhaps the best way to do this is to keep everyone abreast of the visual content to build excitement and anticipation. I have not seen any client (and I realize that is a categorical statement) who is not excited when he or she sees a pencil sketch. It seems odd and intriguing that their company offerings and point of view are forming in front of their eyes in rough pencil sketches. Some of our clients—and we applaud their efforts—go an extra step and package the entire visual scope and strategy. One can take this strategic, scoping sketch and make a piece of print-worthy branded vector art to distribute company wide to pin to walls on their desktops, use as signage, or share on the company extranet. Here is one sample where the planning scoping sketch was turned to vector art.

# FrameConcept's Blueprint for JackBe

**Campaign approach**
This can be designed to live on both a website and interactive PDF that could be emailed or downloaded.

**Value prop video**
This tells a high-level story of why potential customers need JackBe's products and services, including JackBe's Presto. End with link to "Learn More..."

LINKS TO...

**2D infographic series**
This promotes and created interest in JackBe's products. They are data-driven pieces that show how/why.

**Interactive pictogram**
This shows the product process for Presto and variety of uses. Links move through stories for various audiences with technical hows/whys and supporting data.

LINKS TO...

LINKS TO...

| Manufacturing | Finance | Government | Defense | Services | Tech |

**Customer stories**
These can be pointed out in meetings with clients from specific audiences. They tell the pains and gains of the solution for each audience type.

*Links from 2D infographics* can lead to white papers, blog posts, articles, sites, videos, case studies, etc. to support the story with additional insight into the process, market, industry information and research.

- - - - - - - - - - - - - - - - - - - - - - - - - - - - - - - - - - - - - - - - - - - -

The information and visuals can be re-used for PowerPoint/Keynote presentations, trainings, sales meetings, advertisements, brochures, emails, web banners, etc.

◀ *Scoping Sketch Turned To Vector Art for Staff Distibution*

# SELECTING VENDORS: THE LANDSCAPE

- Traditional Options

- Visualizing Visual Options

- 1. Do-It-Yourself Tools

- 2. Infographic Freelancer

- 3. Community Site of Infographic Designers

- 4. Traditional Marketing or PR Agency

- 5. Ad Agency

- 6. Technical Writers

- 7. "Explainer" Video Shop

- Evaluating Information Design Agencies

# TRADITIONAL OPTIONS

# VISUALIZING VISUAL OPTIONS

So you and the organization are convinced that visual solutions are the answer to your business communication goals and you have scoped exactly what type of visual solutions you need short- and long-term. Now you need a vendor. Rather that analyze a particular agency, as agencies can come and go, for the purposes of this book, I thought I would take the reader through the different types of options one might consider. Please remember that I have more than twenty years of experience on the client side so I had first-hand knowledge before I formed an information design agency. My perspective is that there are significant problems with the traditional "normal" options, shown in the following visual and discussed below.

# THE VISUAL SOLUTION
# PROVIDER LANDSCAPE

There is a lot of buzz around leveraging visual content for inbound marketing and communication programs. That's one of the reasons why we put together our own "8 Reasons for Companies to be Visually-Centric." In a very visual way, this sums up the positioning we believe businesses should take.

With a whole host of visual solutions providers out there, both large and small, it can be hard to pinpoint what tools or providers can meet your business goals.

And with each visual solution supplier "type" that one can consider, each of these comes with its own pros and cons.

Our latest infographic takes you through each one of them and provides 7 major concerns you may wish to consider.

## 7 COMMON PITFALLS OF VISUAL SOLUTION PROVIDERS

HOW CAN I SHOW THIS VISUALLY?

 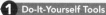 **1 Do-It-Yourself Tools**

There are number of "graphics" and "charting" tools (both free and for fee) whose intention is to allow the non-designer to come up with compelling data visualizations and infographics.

THE CONCERN:
- **Cookie-cutter template designs**
- **Weak on data visualization**
- **Still takes time and resources**

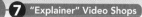 **7 "Explainer" Video Shops**

A cottage industry solution that tends to be aesthetically "kiddy" and more consumer-oriented.

THE PROBLEM:
- **Difficult to communicate complex business data**
- **Can be too childlike - cartoonish**
- **Typically a one-off solution**

 **2 Infographic Freelancer**

Businesses should be concerned about the capabilities and bandwidth of freelancers, competing clients, vacations and interest in your project. These cannot guarantee you the strategic partner you need.

THE PROBLEM:
- **Bandwidth issues**
- **Not a strategic partner**
- **Availability when you need it most**

**6 Technical Writers**

Here the robustness is in spades but the engagement side of the house is lacking. You simply do not have the luxury of your audience pouring through a manual to come to terms with your offering.

THE ISSUE:
- **No engagement factor**
- **Not effective at marketing**
- **Niche audience**

 **3 Community Sites of Infographic Designers**

While the collective portfolio is larger than a single provider, you are still ultimately dealing with one-offs from a community site that places a margin on top of an existing pool of mostly off-shore freelancers .

THE SPIN:
- **Paying for margins**
- **Why deal with middlemen**
- **Long-term potential lacking**

 **4 Traditional Marketing or PR Agency**

Typically will have some "graphics" capability but not from an information designer point of view. There is not the rigor you need for meaningful infographic content.

THE WORRY:
- **Lack of information design**
- **High expense for traditional media**
- **Not robust enough for complex data**

 **5 Ad Agency**

Plenty of sizzle with polished commercial production capabilities but these are typically aimed at the ad and consumer level.

THE CONCERN:
- **Lacking the B2B context**
- **Lots of hype, little substance**
- **Media placement costly**

CALL TO ACTION

# 1. DO-IT-YOURSELF TOOLS

A crop of charting type tools have been developed to answer the need for visual content in the form of infographics. The motivation for those who use these tools is to skip the expense and time involved working with a professional information designer. The results are clunky. With a one-size-fits-all template, there is no hope of coming up with a visual narrative that works with your story. They typically lack finesse and reflect poorly on the brand of the publisher. We spend a lot of time here at Frame Concepts at the beginning of the project with pencil sketches teasing out the narrative to get that nuanced "ah-hah" moment that it's a losing battle to force anyone's unique concept into a preconceived infographic template.

# 2. INFOGRAPHIC FREELANCER

This option—a robust information design agency familiar with your industry nuances and business goals and equipped with the latest technical tools to create the "right" visual application—is close to our recommended solution. But selecting an infographic freelancer falls under the same umbrella as dealing with any freelancer. They are focused on multiple clients with different priorities and may or may not have nuanced knowledge of your industry or marketing practices, and they may not find your business topics interesting. In my client-side days, there were plenty of graphic designers claiming to be information designers because the discipline was "hot" right now.

But my concern is more about the client who is taking this path. How are you getting your marketplace engaged? Do you think doing a single infographic with one freelancer

is going to do the trick? We have developed a case for your organization to be visually centric to get your marketplace and your company onboard with your approach and offerings. A single infographic working with a freelancer reeks of: "Let's try an infographic and see what happens." Such short-sighted approaches are doomed to failure and can cause a lot of damage later when your organization is really ready to jump on the visual content ship and the naysayer from finance says: "We already tried that and that infographic did not move the needle." It's better to work with a team that wants to form a long-term relationship and develop a visual content program that's going to win over your marketplace.

# 3. COMMUNITY SITE OF INFOGRAPHIC DESIGNERS

The community sites of information designers (and I am not going to name names) earns the same critique I had against freelance infographic designers. Sure, you have a wider selection, but it all is predicated on trying out an infographic with an artist whose portfolio you like. It's easy to see why these community sites have sprung up. They want to create an "infographic tool" that they can charge licensing fees for, but it's messy work learning and unpacking clients' offerings and coming up with the design and illustration outputs and edits. The community sites simply put up third-party freelance artists' portfolios, and then the site takes a percentage of the fees paid. It's a clean business model for the community site owner, but we are making a case for your organization to embrace visuals as part of your communication programs.

This doesn't mean a single infographic project you pick up one year and then try again a few years later. It's hard work coming to terms with a client' s nuance offering and advancing educational and engaging infographic content programs that will attract the community to those offerings. I am concerned about the intentions of the client who goes to these community sites (it's clear that the community site's intentions are to make a profit by hosting artists' portfolios). But it is short-sighted on the part of clients to use these sites, just as is sourcing an individual freelancer directly. It suggests that infographics and visual solutions are a bit of a novelty—a one-trick pony—you can create with strangers on community sites effectively. But your business is riding way too much on marketplace understanding and engagement with your offering and your point

of view to play with strangers on a community site. There's no substitute for the hard work involved, and you need a team that will spend time learning your nuances and feed a sustained content program that will win over the marketplace over time.

# 4. TRADITIONAL MARKETING OR PR AGENCY

This is where one goes for creative solutions, right? Well, the information design craft is not where their strengths or even basic capabilities typically lie. You will find that, if you ask the agency for comprehensive visual solutions for your business, the agency will search for vendors themselves. That can work, but often the marketing or PR agency can feel threatened by the information design agency, and you might not receive the best work because they are inserting themselves as the intermediary and putting a margin on top. What you really want is an information design agency that is very integrated and knowledgeable of the nuances of the marketing and PR practice as well as your industry so you can focus on getting the best visual for your offerings and point of view.

# 5. AD AGENCY

This is where one goes for creative solutions, right? Well, the information design craft is not where their strengths or even basic capabilities typically lie. You will find that, if you ask the agency for comprehensive visual solutions for your business, the agency will search for vendors themselves. That can work, but often the marketing or PR agency can feel threatened by the information design agency, and you might not receive the best work because they are inserting themselves as the intermediary and putting a margin on top. What you really want is an information design agency that is very integrated and knowledgeable of the nuances of the marketing and PR practice as well as your industry so you can focus on getting the best visual for your offerings and point of view.

# 6. TECHNICAL WRITERS

Just as ad and marketing and PR agencies do not typically deal with technical nuances of explaining complex offerings, a capable technical writer has this ability in spades. Technical writers not only come to terms with the offering with the client, but detail the inner workings with exhaustive operating manuals. Of course, we want engagement as well, and marketing folks know it's hard enough to get a client to fill out an online form, let alone page through hundreds of pages of a manual. Of course, the intent of the output of the technical writer is for an audience that is not only engaged but has signed and paid for the solution already. Our problem is how to get the audience into nuances of the offering without driving them away. That's exactly where information design, armed with iconography, illustrations, charts and maps, and interactive and animation features, can bring the audience in and engage them.

# 7. "EXPLAINER" VIDEO SHOP

Animated "explainer" video shops have been growing like weeds. There seem to be enough "prosumer" animation tools that one can string a simple 60 to 90 second reel fairly quickly and easily. Here our concern is quality, rather than the category per se. The category is a good one—we create a lot of sophisticated infographic animations here at Frame Concepts—but if I used an adjective to point out what I am seeing (again, I was on the client side for twenty years), it would be "kiddy." It's not just that a lot of the illustration and animation is sophomoric (and it is), but the content approach is not sophisticated. It is like a bunch of youthful non-business types overreacting to the fact that they are dealing with a technical or business topic—and they find it amusing. But that's not your audience. You are fighting in the marketplace feeding trough, and you have a sophisticated buying audience you want to come to terms with the nuanced differentiation inherent in your approach. Most of the explainer videos, like a lot of infographics I see, are giving the craft a bad name. Business subtlety does not come simply from having "after-effects" or any animation software competencies.

# EVALUATING INFORMATION DESIGN AGENCIES

Well, let's advance to an actual information design agency. As the founder and CEO of an information design agency, I have to be careful here. So at a high level, here is a high-level list of questions you may want to consider when evaluating an information design agency:

1. **Sophistication of Design**—perhaps the most straightforward point. You can review their online portfolio to form a judgment here.

2. **Sophistication of Content**—Is their portfolio of clients filled with "light" topics? Remember you are going to be detailing nuances of your offering, and you don't want their eyes glazing over because they don't get you or, even worse, are not interested in your dry content.

3. **Industry and Professional Experience**—you do not want to train them on what an inbound content

marketing program is or a landing page is or your industry or profession. These are the givens, and cracking your content with visuals should be at the forefront. You will want to see visual samples in your industry and applied to your profession to feel comfortable.

4. **Newspaper Tendencies**—there are a lot infographic designers and, yes, infographic design firms from the newspaper industry who realized late in the game that infographics in business are "hot." You want to make sure that they have a basic grasp of what a business going to market is all about. You are not selling a newspaper subscription: you have an offering and a point of view to advance.

5. **Ideation**—some infographic designers reuse artwork from an internal catalog built from previous client work. You want fresh ideation. You want sketches on a blank page developed AFTER your

reference material review, and you want to ideate and make changes with your vendor with live review sessions. If you are getting pretty spot illustrations as your very first deliverable, run for the hills. There must be thinking going on for the creative work to truly illustrate your angle and positioning.

6. **Process**—while recognizing that it's a creative process to make original artwork, you have a timeline and budget. The agency should articulate a repeatable, iterative process and, of course, provide business references.

# MANAGING VENDORS: A REPEATABLE CREATIVE PROCESS

# GETTING THE BEST CREATIVE WITHIN PREDICTABLE TIMELINES

Sounds like a bit of a contradiction, but one wants the most intuitive and engaging visual end-product done on budget and on time. We have developed a repeatable process that balances the need to keep the client in the loop and the project on track while putting our best creative foot forward at each iteration stage. The two key ingredients are the almighty pencil sketch and an iterative process. Let's take a look at the core three-step process and later look at extending a static infographic into other applications, including interactive and animated and data-driven visualizations and applications.

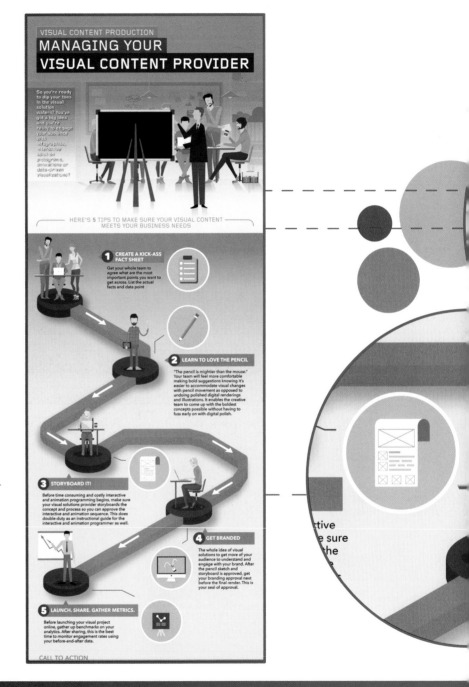

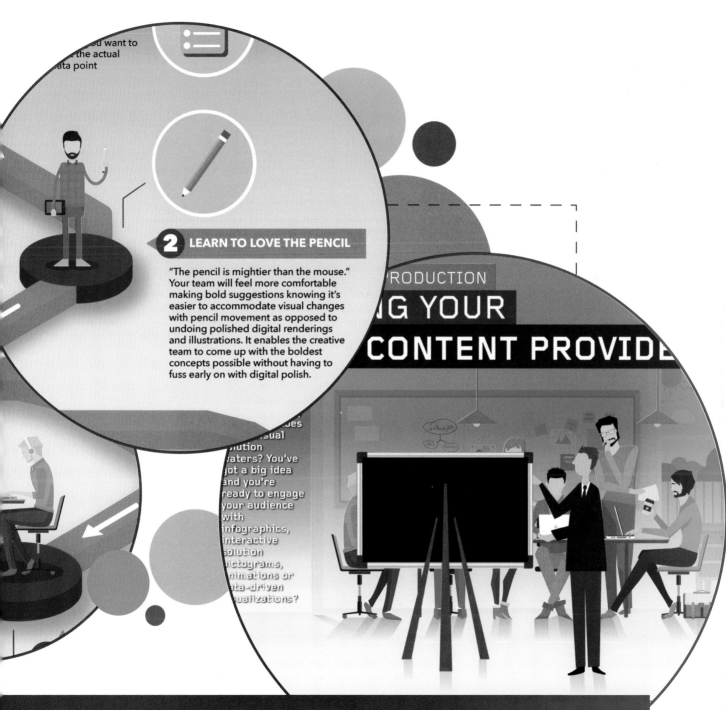

## 2 LEARN TO LOVE THE PENCIL

"The pencil is mightier than the mouse." Your team will feel more comfortable making bold suggestions knowing it's easier to accommodate visual changes with pencil movement as opposed to undoing polished digital renderings and illustrations. It enables the creative team to come up with the boldest concepts possible without having to fuss early on with digital polish.

# PRE-DELIVERY:
# THE OUTLINE

Well before we start on the sketch, it's good to have a clear idea of what the content is about. This includes addressing the audience(s) and their knowledge level, relevant content and data points for the actual infographic content, business goals (awareness, education, conversion, viral sharing, etc.), and details on end-user applications—newsletters, email programs, blogs, trade show signage, websites, sales presentations, brochures, and other uses.

It is important to get the outline and underlying content down before sketching begins. Otherwise, it becomes a two-part and often contradictory hunting mission: "what we are trying to say" and "is the sketch doing a good job of displaying it?" Quite often the problem is tightening down the content so it can fit on one page visually. Typically, anywhere from six to ten key points in the narrative or argument are more than sufficient. If the content is slim—again, not the normal problem—one can leverage large illustrations to bring in an arresting, eye-grabbing image that makes a definitive statement about the key findings. If there is a lot of data, one can make it in more iconic style, using stick people and numbers and charts and maps and data visualization in general to tuck dense data into the final product.

But the hunt for the content is not dissimilar to any content program, whether it is intended for textual blog posts or newsletters. One wants to weave in new angles and perspectives and not make it too "salesy" but—instead—educational, informative, and fun—something your marketplace would like to share but at the same time causes them to consider your approach and your offerings.

On the process side of making an infographic and still on the topic of driving efficiency, it's good to have the outline formed and delivered to the creative team so they can review it and be prepared to discuss different approaches during the kickoff call.

# CONCEPT SKETCH: IDEATION BEGINS

With a tight outline and any relevant reference materials in hand, a kickoff session should be the first actual creative engagement. Here it's good to give your information design team a debriefing about the topic. It's important they hear the tone in your voice, why you care about the topic, and why you want your audience to sit up and take notice.

A good information design consultancy will take you to task. While they are not as close to your subject matter as you are, I hope you have selected a vendor who is familiar with your industry and your profession's business goals (see Chapter 6 on Selecting Vendors). Having led hundreds of these sessions, I have learned that a good supplier will challenge you on your topic and make sure they have the most interesting content on the table to make the most compelling visual. If the vendor is simply listening for instruction from you, then run away (or check your contract on pullout options). You have come for solutions to a communication problem and not to a traditional graphic design agency looking to make your brochure look "professional" or "infographicky." Let your design team repeat back what they are hearing, making sure they are understanding the subtlety of the positioning you worked so hard at. Be prepared to have the important points cataloged into a hierarchy from most important key ideas that the visual will show to supporting points that could be put into a callout box or a footnote.

The end goal of kickoff meetings is to be sure that the lead designer has enough information verbally and written that he or she can come up with a compelling pencil sketch. Once you receive the first pencil sketch is your chance to drive ideation (not at the midnight hour at the end of the project when all the vector art is completed!). You will see in the following simple pencil sketch an analogy and an attempt at putting the core points in the core image and, just as importantly, leaving out the "noise." So you must study the images and the analogy. Are they on point? Are they sophisticated and not insulting to your audience's intelligence level? Were important points left out? Was unimportant content brought to the forefront? Although it's challenging because you are so close to the topic that you automatically can fill in any gaps, stand back and ask yourself whether it is intuitive. Does it advance the case you are trying to make? Perhaps share it with a professional who is knowledgeable about your space, but not so much on nuances of your solution. And whether he or she sees your point(s) through the visual.

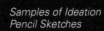

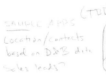

Visual Content Marketing

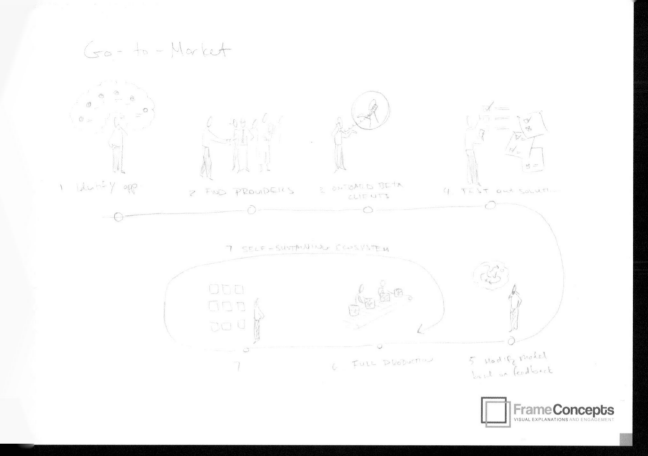

Go-to-Market

1 Identify app
2 Find providers
3 Onboard beta clients
4 Test our solution
7 Self-sustaining ecosystem
6 Full production
5 Modify model based on feedback

FrameConcepts
VISUAL EXPLANATIONS AND ENGAGEMENT

t is important to repeat that this is the tough part—this is the ideation part. It is easy to change a pencil sketch, but changing the core visual approach at the end of say an animation or interactive piece can really upset timeline and budgets. At Frame Concepts our most worrisome response when we deliver and present the first pencil sketch s to receive no feedback and a simple "approved." These are red flags that clients are not reviewing the sketch seriously and perhaps are thinking that they can get to what they "really" think near the end when it's in final, almost publishable form. Again, that upsets the project timing and probably the budget, and it also creates a lesser product. For it is in the debate and pencil sketch quick iteration process that the real creative sparks fly as the client team and information design team work collaboratively to reach the solution that is ideal.

# PARTIAL RENDER

This is a more straightforward and less conceptual stage compared to the pencil sketch ideation phase. Here we are concerned with integrating the visual's look and feel—its brand—to clients' pre-existing brand guidelines or, in the case of startups or larger enterprises new to infographics, help them define their brands. Just as the pencil sketch is to get the concept straight without going too far down the production path, the partial render treats just some of the scenes of the sketch with color and typeface and overall layout.

In the case with the above sample, one of the key sketches in still in the center, but the information designer is developing the brand with color, typeface, and layout treatments around the sketch. This stage is fairly familiar to anyone doing marketing and graphic design in the context of business brand guidelines. But again, it's important to get the brand right before committing to rendering the entire piece. We have seen cases when the brand department was pulled in near the end of the project, and it nixed the core visuals in the final product, turning the process into what was basically a redo.

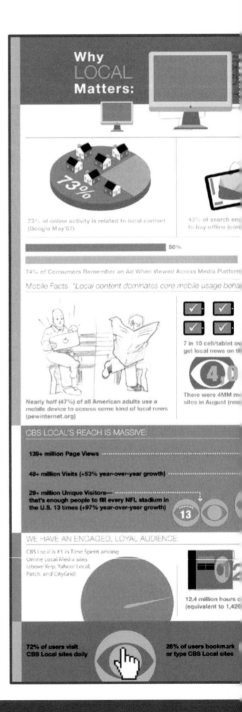

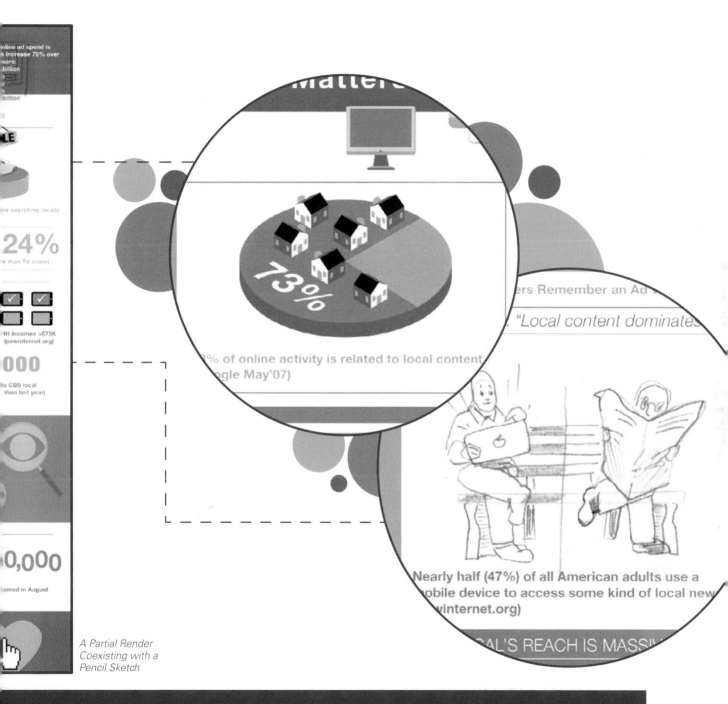

online ad spend is
increase 70% over
ears:
billion

billion

LE

are searching locally

24%
than TV alone)

☑ ☑
☐ ☐
HH Incomes >$75K
(pewinternet.org)

000
to CBS local
than last year)

0,000
amed in August

*A Partial Render
Coexisting with a
Pencil Sketch*

Matters

ers Remember an Ad

"Local content dominates

% of online activity is related to local content
gle May'07)

Nearly half (47%) of all American adults use a
obile device to access some kind of local new
winternet.org)

AL'S REACH IS MASSIV

# FINAL STAGE: FULL RENDER

At this stage, the information design team can, figuratively, go into a cave and complete the project. The pencil sketch and partial render have been approved, so now all the scenes need to be completed. The conceptual design work is done, and quite often your design firm may pass this stage to a rendering team under the guidance of the lead consultant information designer and watchful eye of the design team project manager. There should be no surprises now, and you should feel comfortable, confident, and excited that you have the right solution—and on time. Typical edits at this stage are more likely proofing some of the data points, footnotes, logo, and contact information and any typos. Make sure to get both high- and low-resolution versions for print and web.

# EXTENDING FROM STATIC TO INTERACTIVE, ANIMATION, AND DATA-DRIVEN VISUALIZATION APPLICATION

Here we leverage a storyboard to do double-duty—one to give the client an advance look at how the interactive action will flow and, for animation, how the visual narrative will build over time and, with data-driven visualizations, how the dynamic visualization can be accessed via an integrated user interface. We certainly do not want to cover ground already well trodden by interactive web and user interface design. Instead, we'll talk about sensible ways to integrate the visualization into the process.

# INTERACTIVE STORYBOARD

---

When one makes an interactive infographic or 3D solution pictogram, unlike with a static print piece, one can allow the audience to interact using interactive features such as scroll, page through, zoom in and out, dynamic animation sequences and hyperlinks, call-out boxes, and scene builds, among others. Like a print piece where, through clever information and layout design, one can cajole the eye to scan over the visual so the reader quickly sees the point of the content and is engaged, now we can allow the user to click through and make the experience more immersive. Quite often, we at Frame Concepts do a print piece first and then, with the luxury of interactive, think about how to cut the visual and allow the user to navigate through it in bite-size chunks. But on a practical note, just as the pencil sketch allows a client to see a concept before committing to a final design, an interactive storyboard shows how the designer imagines the user engaging with the visuals and how to keep the important content in the forefront and allow the secondary information to be accessed without diluting the impact of the core points. On a practical note: the approved storyboard can also serve as instruction for the interactive programmer.

As is the case with the above sample, one can use a prototyping tool to allow users to interact with the rough design of (in this case) an interactive pictogram. We find such third-party tools emulate the actual experience better than written instructions and lower the amount of interactive edits once the actual design is programmed for a browser or application format.

**Sitemap**

**Homepage**

Step 1: Who Can Participate?
Step 2: Who funds the account?
Step 3: What are the tax advantages?
Step 4: Eligible Expenses?
Step 5: How to access funds?
Step 6: Investment Options
Step 7: Leftover Funds
Step 8: Rules of the Road
Step 9: Learn More
Step 10: Get Started

## Tax Advantaged Account Tool

HOME | 1 | 2 | 3 | 4 | 5 | 6 | 7 | 8 | 9 | GET STARTED

## Your Tax-Advantaged Account Options

This 3D Pictogram provides a visual representation of the three tax-advantaged accounts that you have access to as an eligible TIAA employee.

To help you decide which account(s) may be advantageous for you to participate in, we have provided you with helpful information on each account, including how and when to use them, what's different and similar, and how to get started.

**Learn More**

**Health Savings Account (HSA)**

**Flexible Spending Account (FSA)**

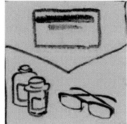

**Retirement Healthcare Savings Plan (RHSP)**

Next: "Who can participate?"

Default (∞)

# ANIMATION STORYBOARD

The animation creation process is quite different, and usually the client is surprised that the first approval milestone is actually the script. The script best describes the entire concept and provides the content that the visual is going to depict and also suggests the pace at which the animation should run. We have found the following order of steps the most efficient process, while giving the client ample time to direct the creative process and keeping the project in scope and on time.

1. Debrief and Reference Material Review

2. Voiceover Script and Edits

3. Pencil Sketch Storyboard and Edits

4. Voiceover and Music Alternate Samples and Selection

5. Digital Render of Approved Pencil Sketch Storyboard and Edits

6. Key Animation Sequence and Edits

7. Full Animation Sequence and Voiceover and Music Syncing and Edits

8. Delivery of Final Animation in Required Format(s)

The following illustration shows a typical voiceover script with animation instructions, accompanied by a pencil sketch storyboard. The next illustration shows how the render will occur before animation programming begins.

## RSA Breach Readiness – Animatic

| Slide | Animation | Voiceover |
| --- | --- | --- |
| 1 | Title slide | What is a CISO's biggest fear? A cyberattack that leads to a damaging breach. |
| 2 | Show data inside of company. Breach opens and data flows out. | The negative consequences of a breach are impossible to recover from: monetary costs, reputational loss, customer loss, and major disruption to the normal course of operations. |
| 3 | Zoom out, show SBIC council | **Breach Readiness** has become a must-have competency for any organization. RSA sought advice from the **Security for Business Information Council** to understand how today's information security leaders build, maintain, and measure their breach readiness.. |
| 4 | Clear stage, animate in and highlight four icons as they are listed | ... and we compared their best practices to more than 170 global respondents from 29 countries, surveying four key areas that contribute to breach readiness: Incident Response Content Intelligence Analytic Intelligence, and Threat Intelligence |
| 5 | Zoom in on Content Intelligence | |
| 6 | Show company with extra walls built around it. Slowly lower extra walls. | Most organizations have acknowledged that a shift away from more preventative controls and tools is warranted, in favor of better capabilities in the areas of **monitoring and response..** |
| 7 | Lower lights and shine on company, expose inside. | Improving **visibility** into what is happening across your environment **is the most important first step** that organizations can take – especially as our infrastructure gets more complex and our attack surface grows. |

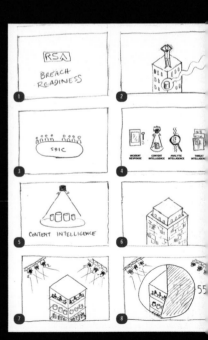

| Slide | Animation | Voiceover |
|---|---|---|
| 8 | Superimpose chart on top of graphic. Animate growth of chart to 55% | However, **55%** of the organizations surveyed still do not have a capability to gather data from across their environment and provide centralized alerting of suspicious activity, rendering them blind to many of today's threats. |
| 9 | Clear stage, show Analytic Intelligence icon | |
| 10 | Superimpose graphic on Analytic Intelligence icon. Highlight growth to 42%. | Further only **42%** of organizations surveyed have capabilities for more sophisticated **network forensics, including packet capture and netflow analysis.** Network and endpoint forensics are invaluable for early detection of more advanced attacks. |
| 11 | Clear stage, show Threat Intelligence icon | |
| 12 | Bring exploit icon from Threat Intelligence bulletin board, fade out rest of bulletin board. Show company interacting with cloud. Highlight data, then show exploit finding a path to the data. | Many damaging breaches have exploited known but unaddressed **software vulnerabilities.** Unpatched perimeter infrastructure is a common entry point for many attacks, and the increasing frequency of broad-scope bugs like Heartbleed and POODLE is making the effort to address vulnerabilities more labor-intensive and more important at the same time. |
| 13 | Superimpose graphic on company. Highlight growth to 40%. | Yet, **40%** of the survey participants don't have **an active vulnerability management program** in place, exposing them to significant risk. |
| 14 | Highlight additional pages from bulletin board, describing multiple exploits. | **External threat intelligence and information sharing** is essential to stay up-to-date on attacker tactics and motives, as well as a good way to speed or shortcut analysis. |
| 15 | Superimpose graphic on scene. Animate growth of negative area of chart, reducing number from 100% to 43%. | Only 43% of organizations surveyed are leveraging an external threat intelligence source to supplement their internal efforts, something which all best-in-class organizations do. |
| 16 | Clear stage. Show Incident Response case icon. | |

| Slide | Animation | Voiceover |
|---|---|---|
| 17-18 | Show pages of plan assembling and being locked into case. | Many organizations have been told that "breaches are a not matter of if, but when." |
| 19 | Superimpose chart on graphic. Animate growth to 30%. | Despite this conventional wisdom, **30%** of respondents in our survey still **do not have a formal incident response plan in place.** |
| 20 | Remove chart, show case aging and getting dusty, cobwebbed. | Lack of established procedures to follow lead to reactive behavior, which makes breach response much less effective. / Regular testing and refinement of response plans is a highly effective practice employed by many leading organizations. |
| 21 | Superimpose chart on graphic. Animate growth to 57% | Among those in our survey who had some sort of IR planning in place, **57% never update or review their plans.** / In the heat of an incident, a plan for potential responders that is well-known and tested can make the difference between a minor compromise and a major loss event. |
| 22 | Clear scene, return to four icons | Firming up these basic building blocks can go a long way to improving your organization's breach readiness. |
| 23 | Show closing slide, call-to-action button | For more information on how RSA can help in your efforts, go to [URL]. |

◀ *Animation Voiceover Script and Animation Instructions*

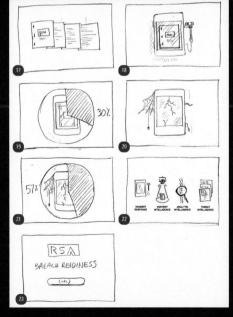

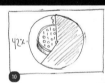
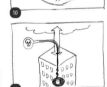

◀ *Animation Pencil Sketch Storyboard*

Animation Artwork Render

Final Animation in Video Player

RSA BREACH6.mov

Incident response

Content Inte...

Analytic ...ence

Threat Intelligence

00:51 — -03:02

Visual Content Marketing

# DATA-DRIVEN VISUALIZATION PROCESS STORYBOARD

Our clients who have experienced the application development process are surprised that, unlike a traditional website or application, the pencil sketch and not a wireframe is the star of the show. Quite often, our clients come to us with problems. They have a "working" interface, but nobody gets it, sees the insights, or is excited about it. We still use wireframes and follow standard iterative web interface development processes and—again—we do not want to go over this well-trodden ground, but would like to talk about putting the all-important visual content and dynamic visualizations into the creative development process. So surprise, surprise, we use pencil sketches even in a robust data visualization development process.

There is a lot of variety with data-driven visualizations. Here at Frame Concepts, we have created

them for projects as wide-ranging as a multimedia timeline for an accounting association to a global risk map to a nuclear reactor spare parts data visualization.

The following pencil sketch storyboards show that pencil sketches can drive the core data visualization concept, as well as how to interact with them in a user interface. On a traditional website, one starts with content from copywriters and then a web designer comes up with the layout and navigation concept. I want to stress with these samples that the visual content—the dynamic visualization—AND the interface are an organic whole and that we come up with the whole concept in the first pencil sketch storyboard phase. Here a few illustrative samples:

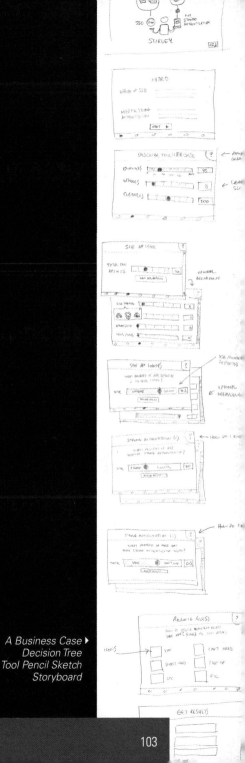

*A Business Case ▶*
*Decision Tree*
*Tool Pencil Sketch*
*Storyboard*

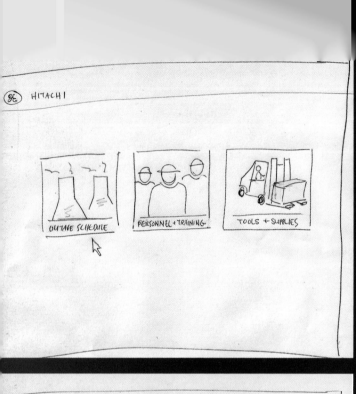

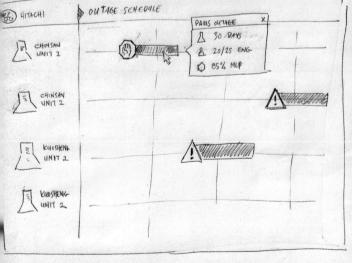

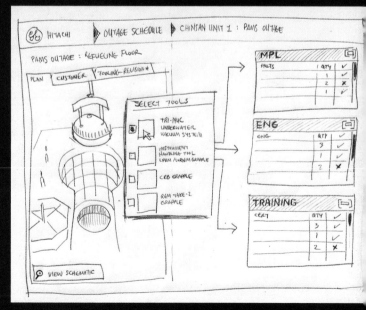

*An Interactive Storyboard for a
Nuclear Reactor Outage Data
Visualization*

**Limit Switch,
3W-59753 Part
No.6, LA-20-6A
LA-80-6**

| system | HCU |
|---|---|
| safety class. | R |
| inventory qty | 10 |
| GEH/HGNE rec. spare qty | 1 |
| manual rec. spare qty | 1 |
| rec. spare qty need | 0 |
| GEH/HGNE rec. outage qty | 1 |
| outage spares need | 0 |
| known obsolescence | n |
| obsolescence solution | n/a |

LEVEL 3 OBSOLESCENCE: 28%
[percentage of obsolescence at each level]

LEVEL 3
no need: 55%
outage need: 15%
obsolescence: 30%

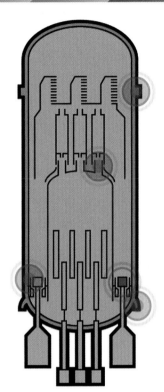

ZOOM 100% ⊕ ⊖

*A Fully Rendered Concept Storyboard for a
Nuclear Reactor Spare Parts Visualization (this was
prospective proposal so went straight to render so
client could imagine the interface)*

# PART 3

# SHOWCASE OF VISUAL SOLUTIONS

# VISUAL SOLUTIONS IN BUSINESS ACTION

We have now seen why visual solutions need to be part of your overall business communication practice, so let's practically look at how to apply them. The range of application is as wide as communications goals and content itself. On a practical level, we have already seen how to scope them into your communications effort with the scoping sketch approach in Chapter 5, Strategy: Scoping in Visual Solutions to Your Organization. We also, as a concept-raising exercise, came up with an infographic suggesting a few ways to apply them.

◀ An Infographic on
Suggestive Ways to
Apply Visual Solutions

# TOP 5
## WAYS TO
## APPLY VISUAL
## SOLUTIONS TO
## YOUR MARKETING
## STRATEGY

E    1/2    F

### t Em
### Onboa

ur team needs to
body the vision and
on of your company -
surprise, surprise -
get them on message.
gaged team aligned to
company's vision gets
the road to a brighter
and will hit your P&L in
a significant way.

d a visual solutions provider that o
•A turn-key    •Complex da
solution    int

gaging visual solution

e consultation &
ration today!
meconcepts.com

### your
### are?"

s "get used to
p them
ow your
unique

tion

### Get Employees
### Onboard

Your team needs to
embody the vision and
mission of your company -
and surprise, surprise -
visuals get them on message.
An engaged team aligned to
your company's vision gets
you on the road to a brighter
future and will hit your P&L in

### Get Clients in th
### Right Frame of Mi

In 60-90 se
prospect with li
knowledge of you
should come to te
should care
inform
a

# THE SHORT ANSWER IS THAT VISUAL SOLUTIONS CAN BE APPLIED EVERYWHERE

Within the scope of this book, we certainly do not want to overlap lessons on what content and product marketing and employee communications and application interface design are, but we want readers to realize that a visual-centric approach using information design is a game-changer for these interfaces. The theme of this book is that these ubiquitous categories of communications and engagement interfaces with the marketplace and employees are in need of the explanatory and engagement lift that information design can bring.

# A PICTURE IS WORTH A THOUSAND WORDS

I have written the balance of this book without using this phrase, but I have noticed when giving presentations and making a sustained argument for visual solutions in business communication and some of the practical steps one can take in onboarding this approach and select and manage creative vendors, my audience gets glassy-eyed. They impatiently want to see the actual visual solutions in play. This makes sense. It's one thing to make a case and come up with a strategy and tactics to bring them into your organization, but another to stand back and see whether they are actually taking hold in the marketplace—and on a more fundamental point: What do they look like in my context?

# VISUAL SOLUTIONS ARE BEING APPLIED EVERYWHERE

Now the narrative of this book takes a different turn. While I have presented a sustained argument for a visually centric approach for business communications and strategic and tactical guidance on getting started and executing, now I suggest in a rather dramatic visual showcase that the train has in fact left the station. While you and your organization are considering the merits of this approach, visual solutions are integrating into business practices. To show how widespread this visual movement within business is, we have sorted our examples into categories, with the goal that every reader will see that this approach is relevant for his or her visual project type, industry, profession, or organization type.

# VISUAL APPLICATION SAMPLES CATEGORY

To make it easier to see applied visual solutions that are relevant for your needs, we have sorted them into categories: Visual Solution, Profession, Industry, and Organization.

Infographics

Interactive Media

Inbound Marketing Programs

Solution Pictograms

Value Proposition Videos

Data-Driven Visualizations

## Visual Solutions by Organization

Startup

Agency

Not for Profit

Enterprise

## Visual Solutions by Profession

Training

Operations

Social Media / PR

Research

Sales and Marketing

Product Development / Programming

## Visual Solutions by Industry

Construction and Real Estate

Education

Energy

Financial Services

Healthcare

HR and Recruiting

Ideation/Product Dev

IT Networking

Management Consulting

Media

Pharmaceutical

Professional Services

Research

Retail and Ecommerce

Software

Technology

Telecommunications

Travel

# INFOGRAPHICS

# FINANCIAL DATA INNOVATION LAB WANTS TO VISUALLY SHOWCASE INNOVATION OUTPUT

An Enterprise Innovation Lab based in New York wanted to showcase how their comprehensive databases of financial information focused in the SMB space could integrate with innovative technology startups to produce impactful marketplace-specific solutions. One of the first innovative integrated solutions spun out of the lab was mProspector—a mobile solution that enabled field sales representatives to walk into any building or down any city street and tell what businesses existed in that building and neighborhood, know key pertinent financial data and staff at that office, and capture any additional information from that visit and load it into the company's CRM tool, all while traveling and using only their smartphones. To tease out the innovation and value inherent in the solution, the client asked to have it visually packaged into the form of a one-page infographic.

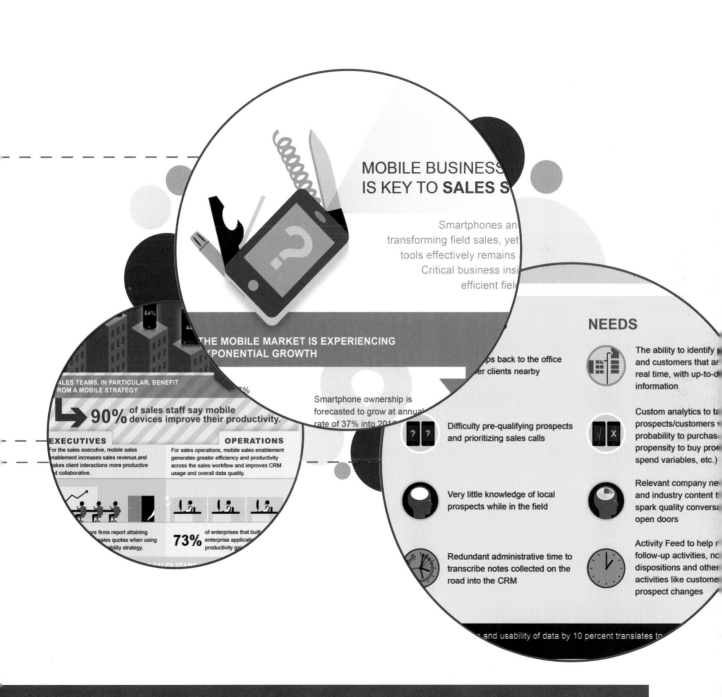

MOBILE BUSINESS
IS KEY TO **SALES S**

Smartphones an
transforming field sales, yet
tools effectively remains
Critical business insi
efficient fiel

THE MOBILE MARKET IS EXPERIENCING
PONENTIAL GROWTH

64%

ALES TEAMS, IN PARTICULAR, BENEFIT
ROM A MOBILE STRATEGY

**90%** of sales staff say mobile
devices improve their productivity.

Smartphone ownership is
forecasted to grow at annual
rate of 37% into 201

**EXECUTIVES**

For the sales executive, mobile sales
nablement increases sales revenue,and
akes client interactions more productive
d collaborative.

**OPERATIONS**

For sales operations, mobile sales enablement
generates greater efficiency and productivity
across the sales workflow and improves CRM
usage and overall data quality.

re firms report attaining
ales quotas when using
bility strategy.

**73%** of enterprises that built
enterprise applicati
productivity ga

## NEEDS

ps back to the office
er clients nearby

The ability to identify
and customers that ar
real time, with up-to-d
information

Difficulty pre-qualifying prospects
and prioritizing sales calls

Custom analytics to ta
prospects/customers
probability to purchas
propensity to buy pro
spend variables, etc.)

Very little knowledge of local
prospects while in the field

Relevant company ne
and industry content t
spark quality conversa
open doors

Redundant administrative time to
transcribe notes collected on the
road into the CRM

Activity Feed to help r
follow-up activities, no
dispositions and other
activities like custome
prospect changes

and usability of data by 10 percent translates to

# LARGE DIGITAL MEDIA COMPANY NEEDS TO SHAKE UP ADVERTISERS DURING AD WEEK WITH ECOMMERCE METRICS

The newly developed digital properties within a relatively new digital division needed to communicate their impressive demographic and ecommerce metrics in a visual way that would attract the big brand ad spending during a major industry Ad Week in New York. In this project, recognizing that the spreadsheets were loaded with impressive data, an infographic was built with a visual narrative and with engaging analogies that drove home the value the digital media firm offers to prospective brands. The visuals were quite the star of the event, as the buyers were used to boring spreadsheets and charts, thus increasing the engagement factor with trade show buyers.

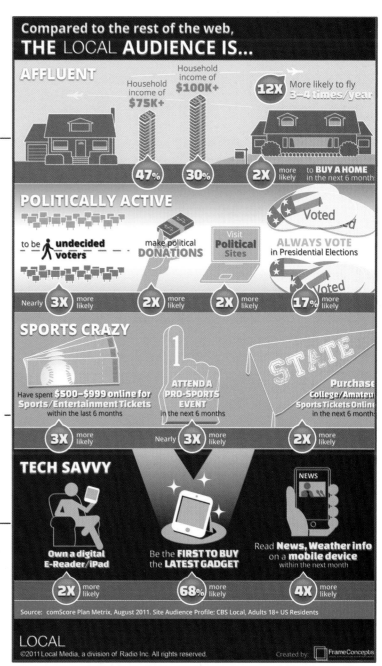

## Compared to the rest of the web,
# THE LOCAL AUDIENCE IS...

### AFFLUENT

Household income of **$75K+**

Household income of **$100K+**

**12X** More likely to fly 3–4 times/year

**47%**

**30%**

**2X** more likely to **BUY A HOME** in the next 6 months

### POLITICALLY ACTIVE

to be **undecided voters**

make political **DONATIONS**

Visit **Political Sites**

**ALWAYS VOTE** in Presidential Elections

Voted

Voted

Nearly **3X** more likely

**2X** more likely

**2X** more likely

**17%** more likely

### SPORTS CRAZY

Have spent **$500–$999 online for Sports/Entertainment Tickets** within the last 6 months

**1** **ATTEND A PRO-SPORTS EVENT** in the next 6 months

STATE

Purchase **College/Amateur Sports Tickets Online** in the next 6 months

**3X** more likely

Nearly **3X** more likely

**2X** more likely

### TECH SAVVY

NEWS

**Own a digital E-Reader/iPad**

Be the **FIRST TO BUY** the **LATEST GADGET**

Read **News, Weather info** on a **mobile device** within the next month

**2X** more likely

**68%** more likely

**4X** more likely

Source: comScore Plan Metrix, August 2011. Site Audience Profile: CBS Local, Adults 18+ US Residents

LOCAL

Created by: FrameConcepts

# PREDICTIVE ANALYTICS FIRM USES INFOGRAPHIC TO DEBRIEF ANALYSTS

A predictive analytics firm wanted to underscore how big data was having an impact on the enterprise's ability to sort through the data deluge. To showcase the need to come up with an analytics solution to effectively perform application performance management (APM) and proactively resolve issues that were buried in the mountains of increasing data, they leveraged an infographic to visualize the number problem. The unusual application for this piece was not the fact that they included it in their website news section but that they effectively used it to debrief research analysts on their problem and their point of view.

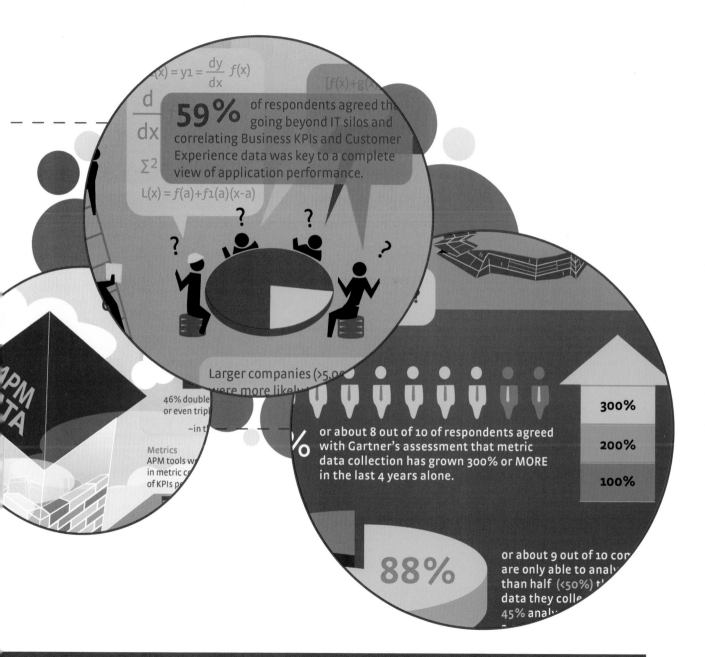

# INBOUND MARKETING PROGRAMS

- Networking Vendor Scope Visual Strategy Around Their Differentiated Offering

- Reputation Consultancy Gets Existing Clients to Appreciate Value of Delivered Offering

- Small Business Health Index Iconic Design Is Integrated with Infographic Content Program

# NETWORKING VENDOR SCOPE VISUAL STRATEGY AROUND THEIR DIFFERENTIATED OFFERING

This networking vendor could diagnose a potential network failure in just three clicks with its innovative offering. The question became how they could leverage an integrated visual communication strategy to increase awareness and conversion on their website. Before creating each of the visual solutions for an integrated go-to-market plan, we stepped back and visually strategized how each visual solution would roll out and integrate with the others. The outcome of that formal exercise was the scoping sketch shown.

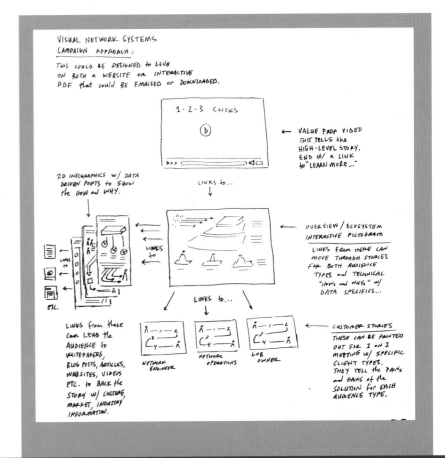

# REPUTATION CONSULTANCY GETS EXISTING CLIENTS TO APPRECIATE VALUE OF DELIVERED OFFERING

The consulting firm can actually report on existing reputation issues and translate that to financial impact if their client does or does not act on their recommendations.

To showcase their findings with a client, they asked to create a compelling visual to present these findings and also to come up with a visual invitation to encourage the

stakeholders within their client's organization to attend the workshop. The following showcases a sample slide and multi-tabbed invite.

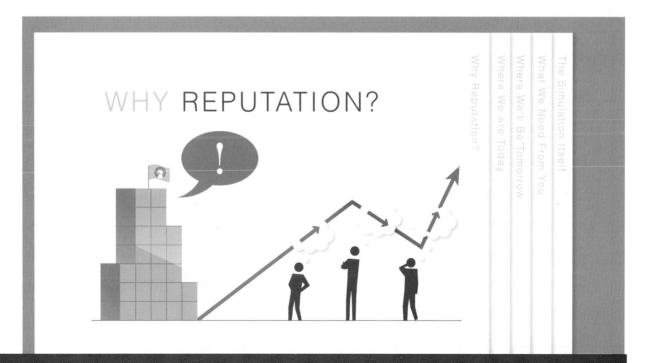

# SMALL BUSINESS HEALTH INDEX ICONIC DESIGN IS INTEGRATED WITH INFOGRAPHIC CONTENT PROGRAM

The client has a comprehensive view on economic health conditions in the small business marketplace, and their ubiquitous industry standard risk number underpins that fact. This infographic leveraged iconography and data visualization to develop a newly designed Health Index Report and coupled that with an infographic series showcasing their robust point of view on all things finance and small business.

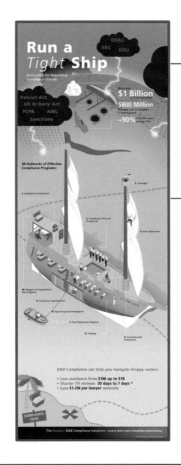

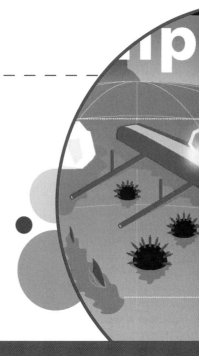

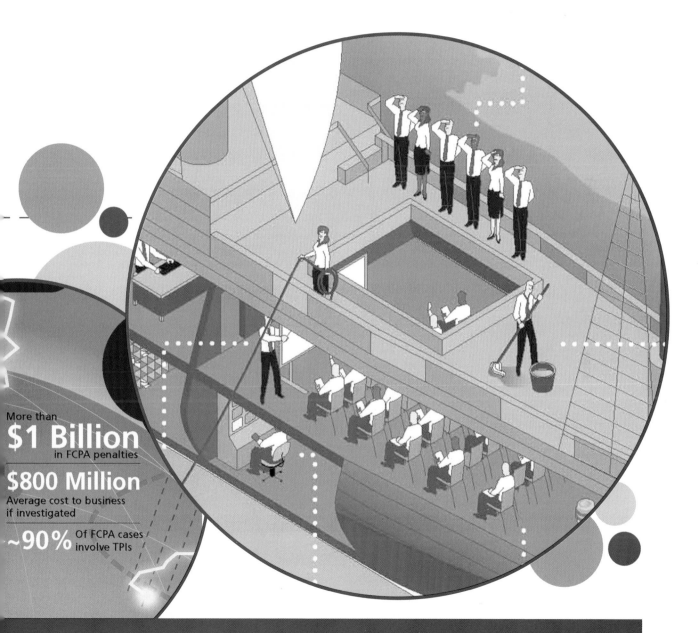

More than
## $1 Billion
in FCPA penalties

## $800 Million
Average cost to business
if investigated

## ~90% Of FCPA cases
involve TPIs

# VIDEO

# ENTERPRISE SOFTWARE ANIMATION TAKES THE AUDIENCE TO THE SEA WITH A COMPELLING DATA MANAGEMENT VISUAL ANIMATION

A global enterprise software vendor wanted to showcase how an integrated approach to data management can drive a business's bottom line while leveraging custom research it had sponsored. To bring research to life, we came up with a concept making clever use of a fishing analogy throughout the video. While this sample breaks the 60- to 90-second rule, it also shows that comprehensive research with an educated audience benefits from information design integrated with a compelling animation movement.

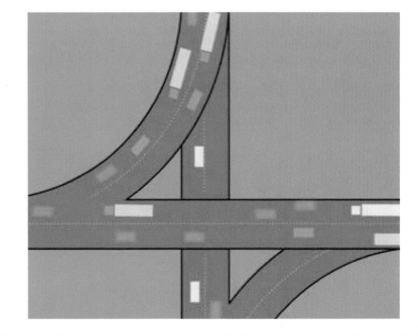

# CLIENT VIRTUALIZATION GETS AN ANIMATED JOURNEY WITH AN INFOGRAPHIC BONUS

Research was leveraged to help its audience appreciate the finer points of taking on client virtualization in the enterprise. In a bit of a production twist, the video production actually started with an infographic that told the journey story in print form and then converted the infographic into a live animation. The two play off nicely from each other and can be used in different applications to reinforce the same message.

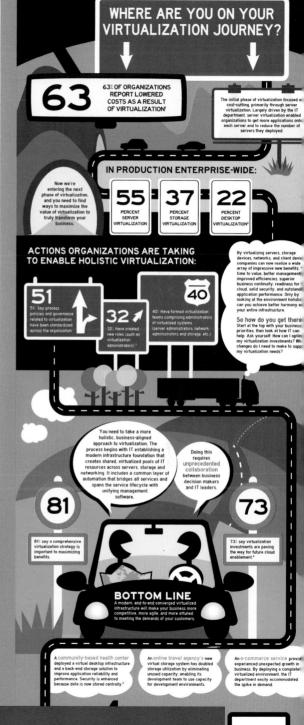

# ENTERPRISE FIRM LETS TRAFFIC ANALOGY DRIVE DATA MANAGEMENT RESEARCH KEY FINDINGS HOME WITH ANIMATION

This animation showcases how data siloes and unstructured data and big data concerns can influence one's ability to effectively manage an enterprise. In this case, a traffic analogy leverages roadways and winding paths and traffic congestion to make the visual point.

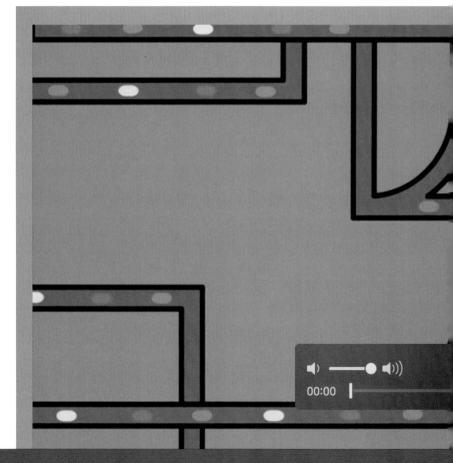

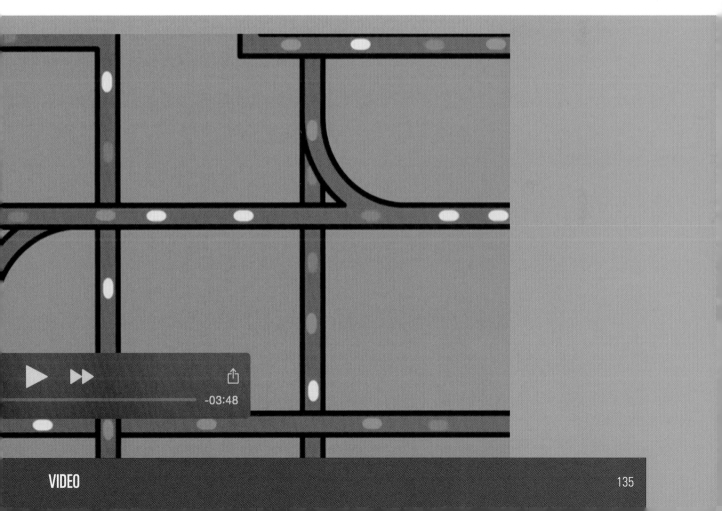

# SOLUTION PICTOGRAMS

- Trading Communications Platform
  Uses Visual Pictogram to Contextualize
  Offering in Trading Lifecycle

- Video Analytics Firm Applies
  Pictogram to Case Study Program

- Networking Solution Company
  Applies Pictogram to Case Study
  Program

# TRADING COMMUNICATIONS PLATFORM USES VISUAL PICTOGRAM TO CONTEXTUALIZE OFFERING IN TRADING LIFECYCLE

The vendor had built a telecommunications platform specifically around the needs of trading houses on a global scale. They wanted to make sure that they were not confused with some of the global telecommunication brands that offered the same generic service for retail, travel, and consumer goods as they did for financial institutions. The client knew their trading audience had very nuanced needs around the trading day and would appreciate the value they built into their telecommunication services. To drive this point home, a visual was created to show how different aspects of the offering integrated with the trading lifecycle. To separate it even further on a brand level, they used a line art type style that stood out from the usual suspects in this space.

# VIDEO ANALYTICS FIRM APPLIES PICTOGRAM TO CASE STUDY PROGRAM

Clever technology was being deployed so this vendor's clients could detect real-time what bottom-line sports signage was delivering on audience awareness. To accomplish this, we created a pictogram that slices each technical layer so the audience can appreciate the innovation and value the solution delivered.

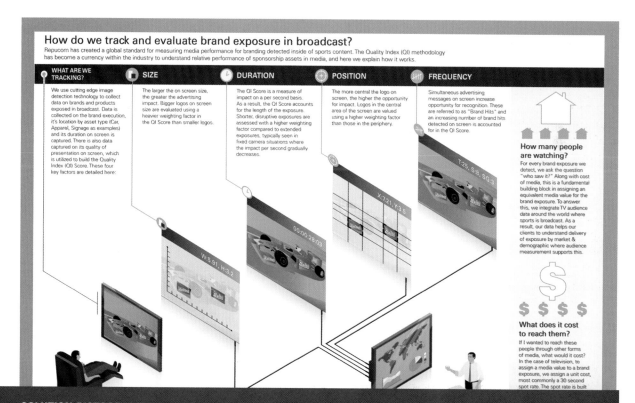

### How do we track and evaluate brand exposure in broadcast?

Repucom has created a global standard for measuring media performance for branding detected inside of sports content. The Quality Index (QI) methodology has become a currency within the industry to understand relative performance of sponsorship assets in media, and here we explain how it works.

**WHAT ARE WE TRACKING?**

We use cutting edge image detection technology to collect data on brands and products exposed in broadcast. Data is collected on the brand execution, it's location by asset type (Car, Apparel, Signage as examples) and its duration on screen is captured. There is also data captured on its quality of presentation on screen, which is utilized to build the Quality Index (QI) Score. These four key factors are detailed here:

**SIZE**

The larger the on screen size, the greater the advertising impact. Bigger logos on screen size are evaluated using a heavier weighting factor in the QI Score than smaller logos.

**DURATION**

The QI Score is a measure of impact on a per second basis. As a result, the QI Score accounts for the length of the exposure. Shorter, disruptive exposures are assessed with a higher weighting factor compared to extended exposures, typically seen in fixed camera situations where the impact per second gradually decreases.

**POSITION**

The more central the logo on screen, the higher the opportunity for impact. Logos in the central area of the screen are valued using a higher weighting factor than those in the periphery.

**FREQUENCY**

Simultaneous advertising messages on screen increase. These are referred to as "Brand Hits" and an increasing number of brand hits detected on screen is accounted for in the QI Score.

**How many people are watching?**

For every brand exposure we detect, we ask the question "who saw it?" Along with cost of media, this is a fundamental building block in assigning an equivalent media value for the brand exposure. To answer this, we integrate TV audience data around the world where sports is broadcast. As a result, our data helps our clients to understand delivery of exposure by market & demographic where audience measurement supports this.

**What does it cost to reach them?**

If I wanted to reach these people through other forms of media, what would it cost? In the case of television, to assign a media value to a brand exposure, we assign a unit cost, most commonly a 30 second spot rate. The spot rate is built

## NETWORKING SOLUTION COMPANY APPLIES PICTOGRAM TO CASE STUDY PROGRAM

The client wanted to showcase some of the industry-specific value they had been delivering in the form of a case study with a provocative large visual to grab the eye. In the following sample, the shipping industry was a focus and, with the explanatory visual guiding the way, the client made its case that their networking troubleshooting solution was able to perform root cause problem sourcing regardless of the shipping network issue.

MSC Home Terminal is one of Eu
requirements for their key applica
components ranging from aspects
container damage, badge readers
Managing and troubleshooting ap
related problems was growing in

TruView Visibility

# View *keeps*
# ON THE MOVE

s busiest container terminals. Managing the
s extremely difficult because it is made up of different
desktops, cameras for number plate recognition and
thin clients, and more.
tion an network-
lexity.

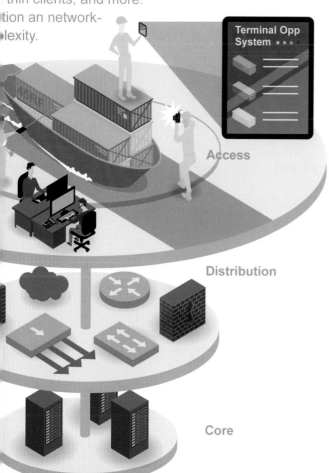

Access

Distribution

Core

## SHIPPING, LOGISTICS, AND TRANSPORTATION

### Challenge

Visibility into performance issues had a serious
impact on the charging and discharging of cargo from
the vessels, trains and trucks.

### Solution

Visual TruView™ Appliance

### Result

IT team now has an comprehensive view of overall
performance which has led to faster problem isolation
and troubleshooting, and lessened the risk of service
impacting performance related issues.

"Before we deployed the TruView, we lacked an
independent overview tool which led to longer times
to identify and pinpoint the culprit.  Instead of focusing
on a single area, we now had a complete view of
performance across the entire application and network.
This helped us find problems faster, regardless of
where they were occurring."

-Tamara Lievens, ICT Infrastructure
Manager for MSC Home Terminal

# INTERACTIVE SOLUTION PICTOGRAMS

# SOCIAL RECRUITING PLATFORM GETS INTERACTIVE VISUAL EXPLANATORY LIFT

A leading job board distribution platform was launching its new Social and Mobile Networking Platform and wanted to show conceptually what this new solution allowed its clients to do. However, the client wanted to ensure its customers that its traditional job board distribution platform was still its core offering and that the new solution ran its analytics through the same reporting tool so each channel's performance could be measured. To up the engagement factor even further, in addition to interactive explanatory text boxes, an animation sequence was integrated so at the touch of button, one can see the path of the job requisition.

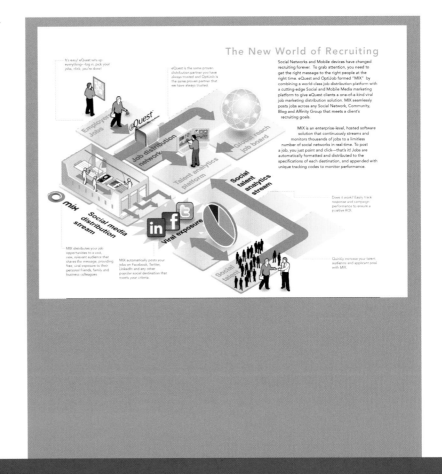

# CONSTRUCTION FIELD SOFTWARE STARTUP SHOWS EFFICIENCIES IMPROVEMENT IN VISUAL BEFORE AND AFTER PICTOGRAM

This startup wanted to reinforce that traditionally all the stakeholders in a large new construction project did not have transparency into the actual build, retrofits from blueprint and spare parts supply issues. This visual solution interactively show the difference between the field software solution installed on tablets and laptops in the field and a traditional model with paper only. They decided to leverage the inter-active storyboard by showcasing, with a split screen, the original plan and new value from the perspec-tive of each stakeholder: Architects, Contractors, Field Crew, and Building Managers. The pictogram highlighted this by placing them in the bottom clickable row below the visual.

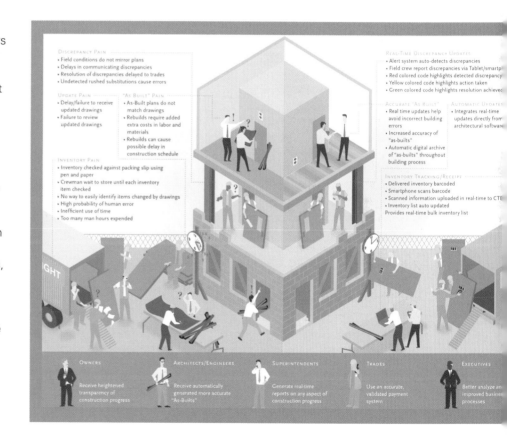

# TRADING COMMUNICATIONS PLATFORM

The core distinctive benefits are converted into clickable buttons in the bottom left corner to unpack different instructional scenes in concert with text boxes that link to more detailed technical information, all while showing the relationship and benefit to the front, middle, and back office of the trading floor.

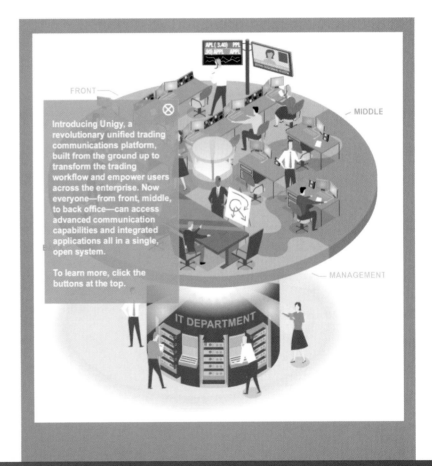

# DATA-DRIVEN VISUALIZATIONS AND APPLICATIONS

- Nuclear Spare Parts Division Needs to Visually Cause Their Clients to Order Spare Parts

- An Accounting Association Celebrates 125-Year History with Tablet Data-Driven Visual Timeline

- Healthcare Managed Service Provider Trains Its Stakeholders the Best Service Delivery Framework with Visual Interactive Card Training Game

# NUCLEAR SPARE PARTS DIVISION NEEDS TO VISUALLY CAUSE THEIR CLIENTS TO ORDER SPARE PARTS

There are not a lot of new nuclear reactors being built, but there are legacy reactors that require spare parts to be stocked and replacement parts for obsolete items to be engineered. However, the nuclear reactor clients were forced to go through reams and reams of spreadsheets to determine what the status of each part actually was. In this project, a prototype was developed to visualize spare parts status for both the nuclear reactor and the control room. The key was a red pulsating point that dynamically allowed the client to navigate quickly to the spare part concern and see a visual of the actual part in question and what its status was. Once the client's client was onboard with the approach, then a full stack data-driven and browser-compatible data visualization application was both designed and developed. But the key driver at the ideation stage was the pulsating point.

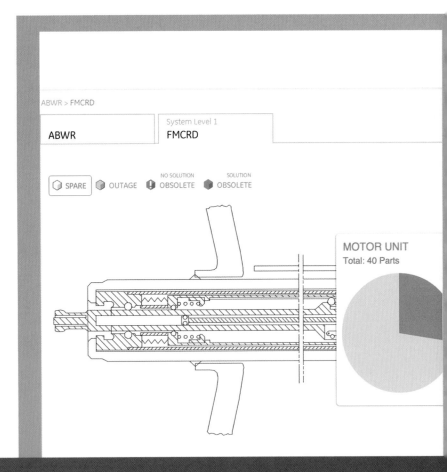

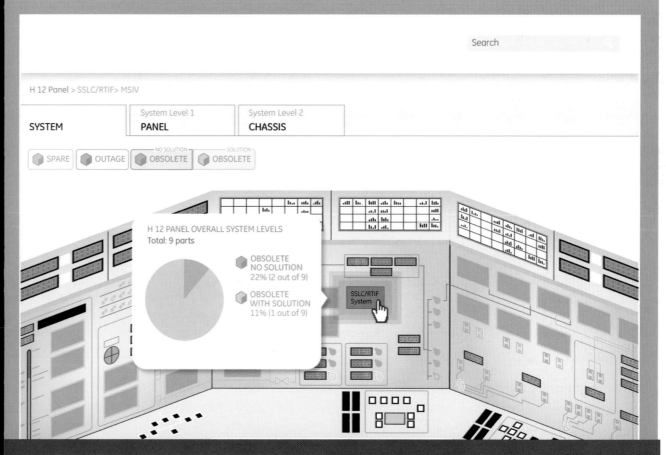

# AN ACCOUNTING ASSOCIATION CELEBRATES 125-YEAR HISTORY WITH TABLET DATA-DRIVEN VISUAL TIMELINE

The Association had a wealth of historic milestones and visual highlights, including photos and videos that they wanted to showcase in an interactive timeline. A data visualization application was developed for desktop and tablet that could load each of the milestones and relevant visual artifacts and built an interactive timeline that allowed a finger to slide to any timeline and quickly pull up an interesting milestone with the relevant visual assets. Because it was a data-driven visualization, the client could simply update the milestones on the spreadsheet and the application would pull from new milestone content each year.

# HEALTHCARE MANAGED SERVICE PROVIDER TRAINS ITS STAKEHOLDERS THE BEST SERVICE DELIVERY FRAMEWORK WITH VISUAL INTERACTIVE CARD TRAINING GAME

The client had refined its service delivery model and wanted to bring its employees and stakeholders into the conversation by interactively work-shopping the optimum process delivery model for their managed healthcare services. The interaction was in a training room format, also soliciting feedback from staff in the field to continuously make training improvements. The game was developed to allow the facilitator to play process cards in any order to interact with each class not in a prescribed order but to allow best practices to emerge with a healthy discussion occurring over the digital game board.

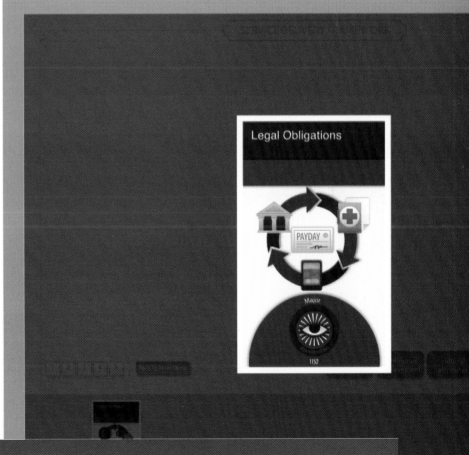

# STARTUP ORGANIZATIONS VISUAL SOLUTIONS

- Large Construction Projects Software Startup Engages with Interactive Pictogram

- Meeting Software Platform Startup Shows Business Inefficiencies in Traditional Meetings

- Innovative Startup for Movie Industry Showcase New Model

# LARGE CONSTRUCTION PROJECTS SOFTWARE STARTUP ENGAGES WITH INTERACTIVE PICTOGRAM

Traditionally large construction projects—like aircraft hangars, warehouses, or nuclear submarines—involve a lot of retrofitting in the field. With static drafting documents, the stakeholders—construction managers, business owners, facilities management, field technicians, and architects—can be left out of the loop. This startup offers transparency on the actual build, and the parts inventory is provided real-time, as shown in this innovative before-and-after interactive pictogram created in HTML5 and JavaScript so it could play on IOS devices like the iPad.

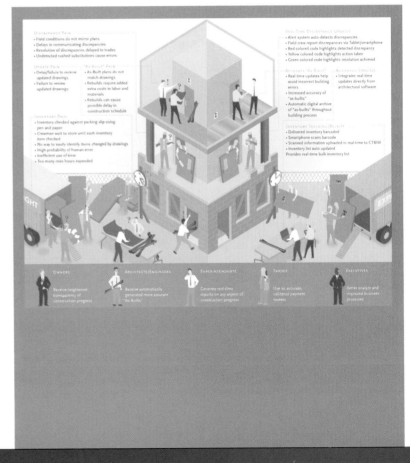

# MEETING SOFTWARE PLATFORM STARTUP SHOWS BUSINESS INEFFICIENCIES IN TRADITIONAL MEETINGS

While this infographic lets numbers tell the visual story, because the startup software platform was designed to make meetings more efficient, the infographic was designed in an actual traditional meeting room to makes it case. Note that, as opposed to a pictogram, which is an explicit visual explanation of the value of the offering, with the infographic, there is a subtle suggestion that the audience needs to rethink how it runs meetings and learn how clients can actually solve the problem.

# INNOVATIVE STARTUP FOR MOVIE INDUSTRY SHOWCASE NEW MODEL

A new film financing platform came up with a clever idea to introduce the latest digital film projector technology in the independent film market and make investors integrated to fund and see return in this provocative alternative investment class. This infographic is actually a blend of infographics showing the numbers side of the business and borrows from the pictogram visual solution by showing how the parts fit together to deliver value to each stakeholder.

## OPPORTUNITY

| Industry-wide shift to digital | Art house theatres: Can't afford digital equipment | Filmmakers: Need meaningful distribution | Neglected market niches | State tax credits |

## INVESTMENT

# $28M TO THE FLOWER CITY FILM FUND

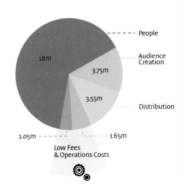

- - - - - People

Audience Creation
3.75m

3.55m

- - - Distribution

1.05m - - - - - 1.65m

Low Fees & Operations Costs

18m

**PROJECTS**

Will have a compelling s
to attract bankable talen
identifiable niche audier
and other leveraged elem
attached.

**AUDIENCE**

Niche audiences
marketed to an
day one of prod
generate anticip
for each film.

**DISTRIBUT**

All films will hav
agreement with
Digital for an ex
engagement w
across the coun

A **low** risk, **high** reward motion picture investment opportunity to produce and acquire up to **15** films to be distributed to **100** theatres across the country.

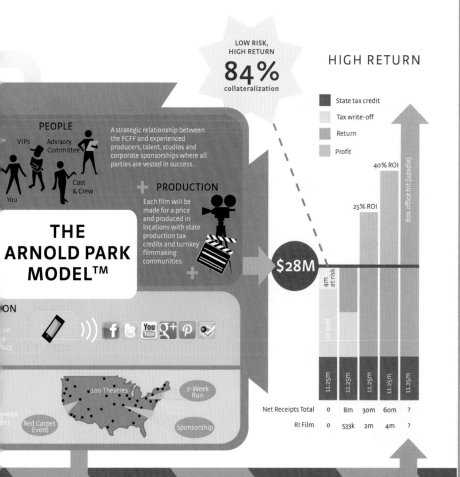

LOW RISK,
HIGH RETURN

# 84%
collateralization

HIGH RETURN

- State tax credit
- Tax write-off
- Return
- Profit

40% ROI

25% ROI

Box office hit (upside)

$28M

4m at risk

12.32m

11.25m   11.25m   11.25m   11.25m   11.25m

PEOPLE

VIPs   Advisory Committee

Cast & Crew

You

A strategic relationship between the FCFF and experienced producers, talent, studios and corporate sponsorships where all parties are vested in success.

PRODUCTION

Each film will be made for a price and produced in locations with state production tax credits and turnkey filmmaking communities.

## THE ARNOLD PARK MODEL™

100 Theatres   2-Week Run

Red Carpet Event   Sponsorship

| Net Receipts Total | 0 | 8m | 30m | 60m | ? |
|---|---|---|---|---|---|
| RI Film | 0 | 533k | 2m | 4m | ? |

**$1.2M PROJECTED NET RECEIPTS PER FILM FOR BOX OFFICE ONLY**

# AGENCY ORGANIZATION'S VISUAL SOLUTIONS

- SEO Agency Leverages Infographic to Drive Their Client's Traffic

- Marketing Automation Consultancy Automates the Understanding of Their Processes

- Branding Agency Leverages iPad Dynamic Timeline Data Visualization

# SEO AGENCY LEVERAGES INFOGRAPHIC TO DRIVE THEIR CLIENT'S TRAFFIC

An SEO agency leveraged an insightful infographic for their client, a residential security provider. This particular infographic focused on FBI crime statistics around home break-ins and was not an explicit promotion of their client's offering. Instead, it artfully raised the concern that one should consider or re-consider one's approach to protecting home valuables. This infographic helped the SEO agency drive traffic numbers for their client to help the client hit their bottom line.

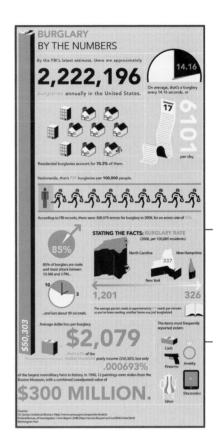

### Outline Ideas

1. How about does a break-in look like – average value, popular items, where they break in. Favorite items include: cash, jewelry, laptops, guns, digital cameras, small electronics (Ipods, GPS, PDA's MP-3's and CD's). Money is usually used to support a drug habit. Breakin typically takes 60 seconds or less.

2. When do most break-in occur?
Usually occur in the daytime when occupants are at school or work.
July and August most the frequent months for break-ins.
February is the least frequent for home breaks.

3. How are homes targeted?
Simple selection process
Choose an unoccupied home with easy access, the greatest amount of cover and the best escape routes.
Homeowners often make this selection process easy for thieves by failing to take simple precautions.

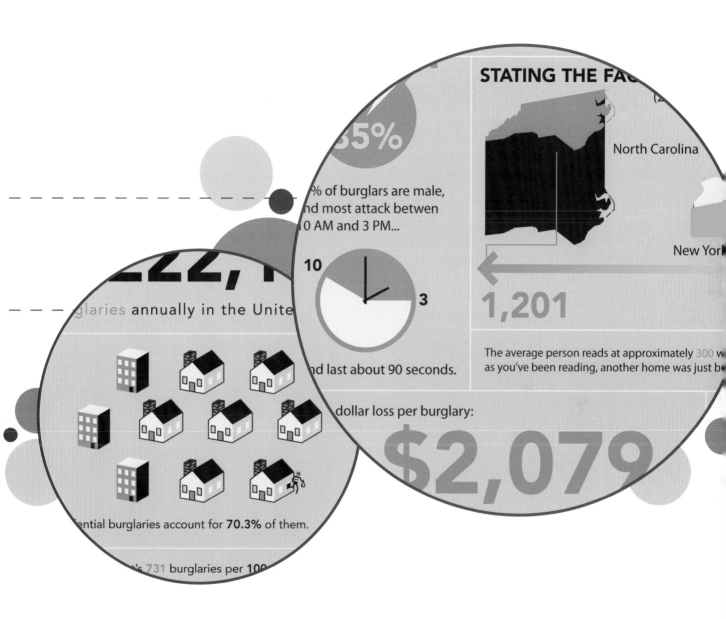

STATING THE FAC

North Carolina

New Yor

% of burglars are male,
nd most attack betwen
0 AM and 3 PM...

10

3

1,201

nd last about 90 seconds.

The average person reads at approximately 300 w
as you've been reading, another home was just b

dollar loss per burglary:

$2,079

glaries annually in the Unite

ntial burglaries account for **70.3%** of them.

's 731 burglaries per 100

# MARKETING AUTOMATION CONSULTANCY AUTOMATES THE UNDERSTANDING OF THEIR PROCESSES

There is science and art to providing an effective marketing automation program. Exactly how this is set up with the complexity of marketing automation software platforms and nuanced client-specific workflows and content refinement can make it difficult for clients to see what they are actually paying for. A marketing automation consulting firm was asked to create an explanatory process pictogram so their prospects (and their clients) could see the rigor and value in their consultative process.

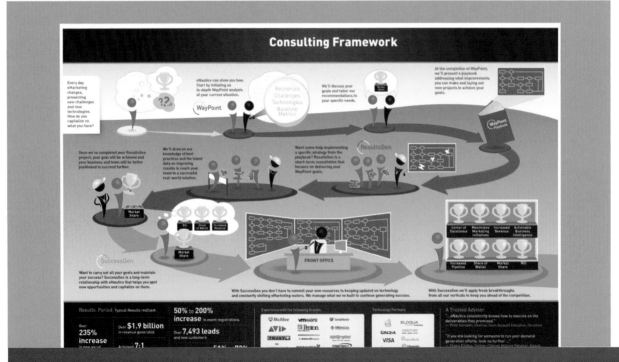

# BRANDING AGENCY LEVERAGES IPAD DYNAMIC TIMELINE DATA VISUALIZATION

While steering the overall brand for an accounting association, a branding firm had a specific request for a dynamic visualization of the historic milestones to celebrate the Association's 125th anniversary. This was built in both HTML5 and Flash to accommodate IOS devices like the iPad as well as older desktop browser versions. The result was a very dynamic visualization of key milestones that included interactive pop-ups for historic videos and photographs.

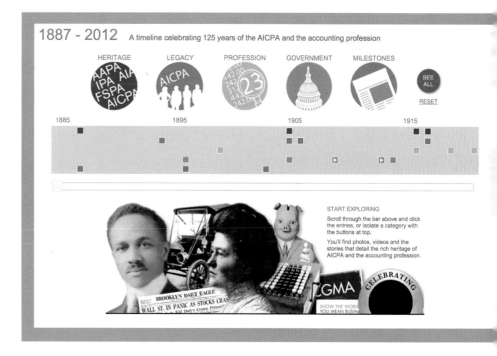

# NOT FOR PROFIT ORGANIZATIONS VISUAL SOLUTIONS

- Children and Widow Charitable Organization
- Architectural Association Showcases Value to Community

# CHILDREN AND WIDOW CHARITABLE ORGANIZATION

A children's charity presented annually to its constituents on how donation dollars were transforming the lives of the underprivileged children and widows it served. In particular the charity was delivering dental kits for children and housing for widows. Through clever use of iconography, the client was able to show how their impact on the lives of children and widows have been increasing year by year.

## Widows' Program

On average, we provide all living expenses for 21 widows every year, for the remainder of their lives.

We pay for each widow's living accommodations, food, medical care and more at Texas Masonic Retirement Center.

## Children's Program

We help children with medical treatment, dental services, autism therapy, educational assistance, and other services.

| 2004-2005 | 2005-2006 | 2006-2007 | 2007-2008 | 2008-2009 | 2009-2010 | 2010-2011 |
|---|---|---|---|---|---|---|
| 120 Children | 100 Children | 31 Children | 800 Children | 1,100 Children | 1,405 Children | 937 Children |

♀ = 20 Children

Note: Some children received services in more than one category

# ARCHITECTURAL ASSOCIATION SHOWCASES VALUE TO COMMUNITY

Architects deliver and direct an indirect value to the community in obvious and not so obvious ways. The association wanted to impress this fact at a major lobbying event in Washington, D.C. But it also wanted to make sure that this infographic poster would be taken under the arm of its lobby group and congress members to be shared with their colleagues. The solution came in the form an infographic posted with an architectural theme and designed so it could fold easily to be carried away from the event.

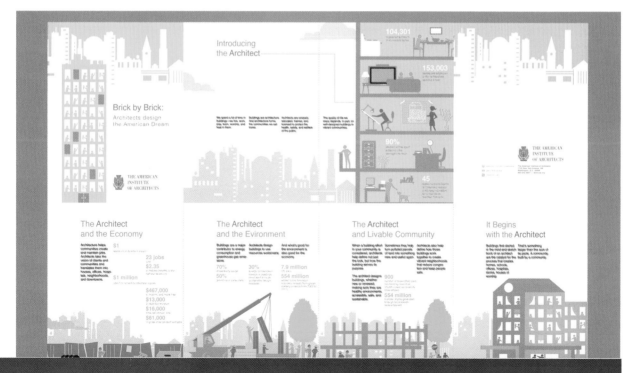

# ENTERPRISE ORGANIZATIONS VISUAL SOLUTIONS

- Nuclear Energy Spare Parts Provider Engages Its Clients with Data-Driven Visualization Tools

- Financial Data Firm Showcases Financial Data Innovation with Infographic Series

- Network Performance Monitoring Solution Visualizes How Process Delivers Business Value

# NUCLEAR ENERGY SPARE PARTS PROVIDER ENGAGES ITS CLIENTS WITH DATA-DRIVEN VISUALIZATIONS TOOLS

The client took innovation one step further by creating a dynamic data visualization of spare parts for both the nuclear reactors and their control rooms so its clients can quickly determine their spare parts inventory status in real-time. The innovative visual communication platform also received a brand lift with new logos that carry on clients' brand identity while subtly reinforcing the innovation inherent in the visual applications.

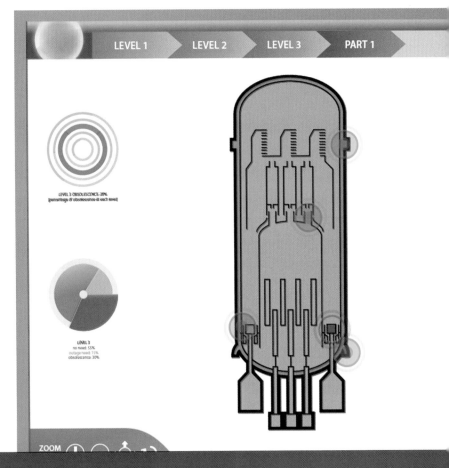

**Limit Switch,
3W-59753 Part
No.6, LA-20-6A
LA-80-6**

| | |
|---|---|
| system | HCU |
| safety class. | R |
| inventory qty | 10 |
| GEH/HGNE rec. spare qty | 1 |
| manual rec. spare qty | 1 |
| rec. spare qty need | 0 |
| GEH/HGNE rec. outage qty | 1 |
| outage spares need | 0 |
| known obsolescence | n |
| obsolescence solution | n/a |

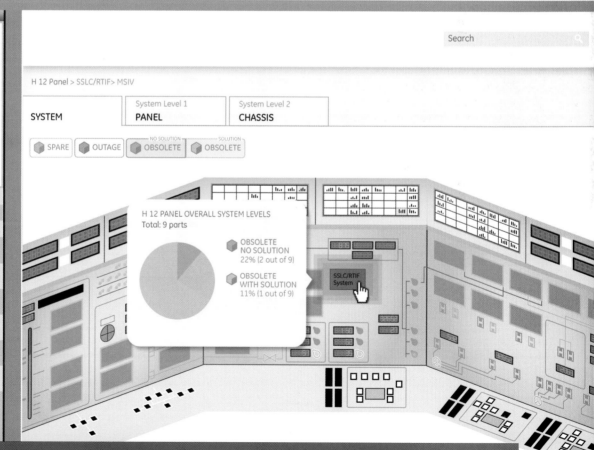

H 12 Panel > SSLC/RTIF> MSIV

**SYSTEM**

System Level 1
**PANEL**

System Level 2
**CHASSIS**

SPARE    OUTAGE    NO SOLUTION OBSOLETE    SOLUTION OBSOLETE

**H 12 PANEL OVERALL SYSTEM LEVELS**
Total: 9 parts

OBSOLETE
NO SOLUTION
22% (2 out of 9)

OBSOLETE
WITH SOLUTION
11% (1 out of 9)

SSLC/RTIF
System

# FINANCIAL DATA FIRM SHOWCASES FINANCIAL DATA INNOVATION WITH INFOGRAPHIC SERIES

The client has a unique status with its proprietary risk number and related financial metrics. The client showcased the value in their data offering with a provocative infographic series that included a new integrated mobile prospecting tool and a visual Small Business Health Index.

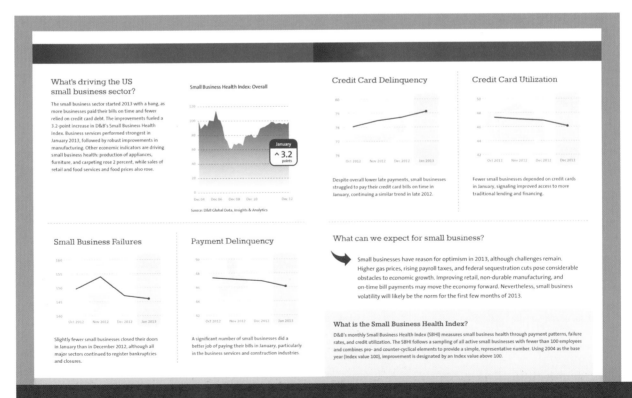

# NETWORK PERFORMANCE MONITORING SOLUTION VISUALIZES HOW PROCESS DELIVERS BUSINESS VALUE

A networking firm can perform a root cause analysis on potential performance issues in only three clicks. The inherent business value needed to come out in their marketing communications, so they had an information design firm create an integrated package that first started with a scoping sketch to tie all the visual pieces together.

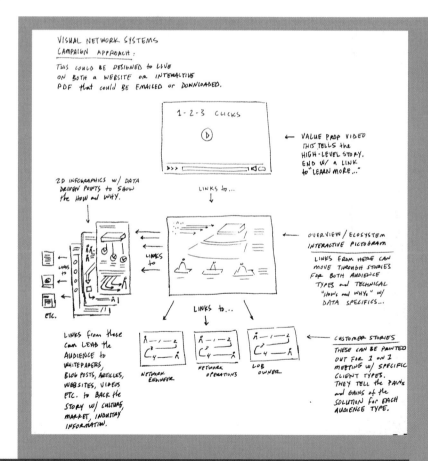

# TRAINING AND CHANGE MANAGEMENT VISUAL SOLUTIONS

- Managed Health Services Provider Trains Its Staff with Interactive Application

- Trading Analyst Training Agency Leverages Pictogram to Show Competency Gaps

- Sales Training Consultancy Shows Transition to Solution from Product

# MANAGED HEALTH SERVICES PROVIDER TRAINS ITS STAFF WITH INTERACTIVE APPLICATION

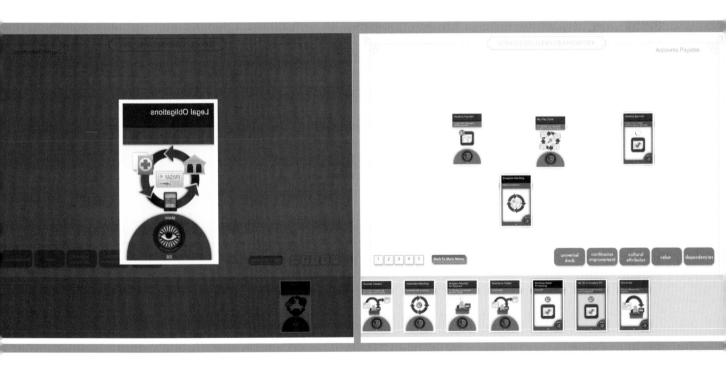

With new management in play and a new optimized managed service delivery created and ready to roll out, the client needed to bring its employees onboard. Rather than prescribe the service delivery steps, the training staff brought everyone onboard by driving the class with an interactive card playing game where the staff (collectively with the trainer) came to terms with the optimal service delivery path.

# TRADING ANALYST TRAINING AGENCY LEVERAGES PICTOGRAM TO SHOW COMPETENCY GAPS

The client had a unique training method to deliver real-world analyst competencies. It also had a unique method to allow its potential students to take a competency test online to quickly determine where their weaknesses were. The challenge was to map how the core competencies related to the performance areas of the working analyst. The following pictogram walks prospective students through the process.

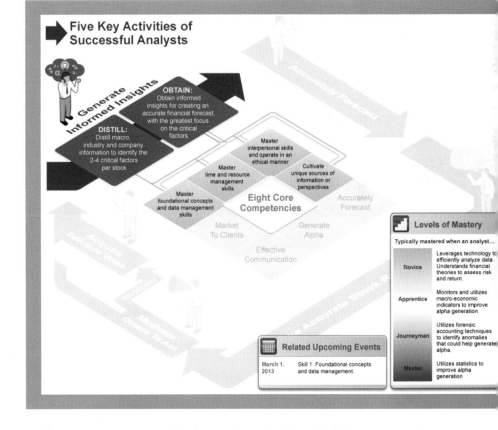

# SALES TRAINING CONSULTANCY SHOWS TRANSITION TO SOLUTION FROM PRODUCT

The challenge in this particular visual explanation was not to reveal the proprietary selling methodology (you have to pay for that) but to reveal enough to show them they were not a typical sales training shop—that trainees could take the sales class from "box pusher, feature sales" to business value, solution sales consultants. We accomplished this by showing tiered levels representing the sales person, the "speeds and feeds" cellar, and rising to the C-level business issue selling suite.

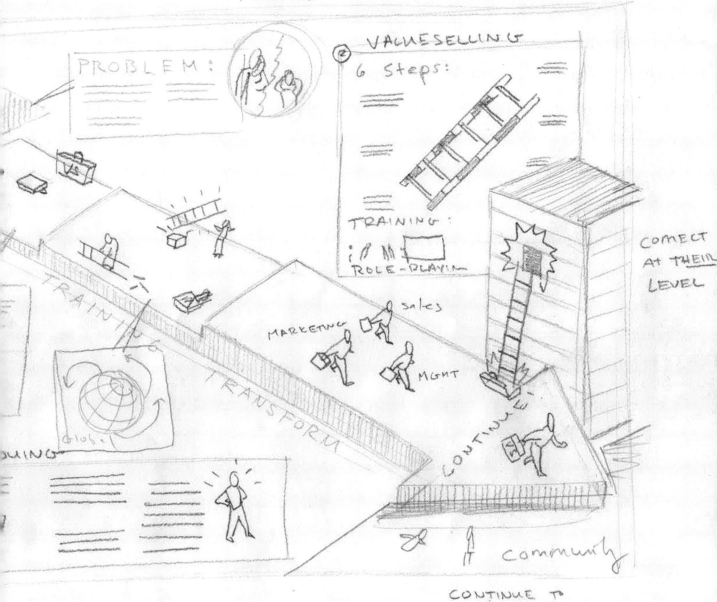

FAILURE TO CONNECT

PROBLEM:

VALUESELLING
6 Steps:

TRAINING:
ROLE-PLAYING

CONNECT AT THEIR LEVEL

TRAINING

TRANSFORM

Global

MARKETING

sales

MGMT

CONTINUE

IT community

CONTINUE TO USE IT

emails

# OPERATIONS AND SUPPORT VISUAL SOLUTIONS

- Canadian Telecommunications Provider Enables Its Clients to Appreciate Its New Platform of Integrated Data Services

- Data Reconciliation Offering Gets Its Clients Onboard with Integrated Visual Solution

- Video Analytics Firm Demonstrates the Social Effect of Super Bowl Ads with Data Visualization

# CANADIAN TELECOMMUNICATIONS PROVIDER ENABLES ITS CLIENTS TO APPRECIATE ITS NEW PLATFORM OF INTEGRATED DATA SERVICES

The client, on the heels of a new service offering, was challenged to visually show how the new suite of services integrated with their operational delivery process steps while also listing their tiers of data services. To solve this communication problem on a single page, a pictogram was created that integrated process steps, tiers of services, and the individual data services—first in a static brochure and presentation and then as an interactive learning experience.

MIGRA

DESIGN

Manag
Servic

Cloud

Data C
Servic

PROFESSIONAL SERVICES

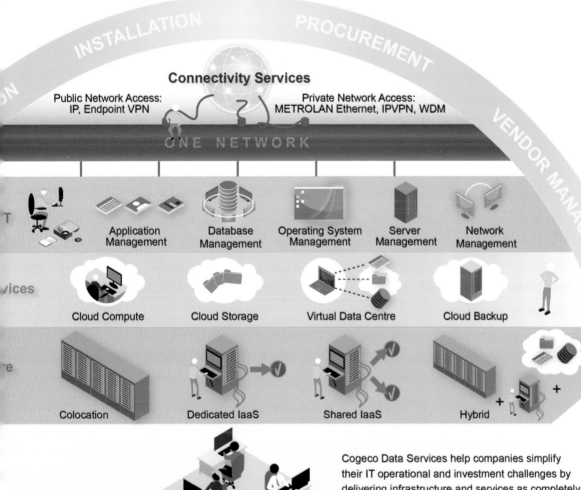

## Connectivity Services

Public Network Access:
IP, Endpoint VPN

Private Network Access:
METROLAN Ethernet, IPVPN, WDM

ONE NETWORK

INSTALLATION

PROCUREMENT

VENDOR MANAGEMENT

PROFESSIONAL SERVICES

Application Management

Database Management

Operating System Management

Server Management

Network Management

Cloud Compute

Cloud Storage

Virtual Data Centre

Cloud Backup

Colocation

Dedicated IaaS

Shared IaaS

Hybrid

YOUR ENTERPRISE

Cogeco Data Services help companies simplify their IT operational and investment challenges by delivering infrastructure and services as completely managed services — enabling alignment of business goals and IT, and allowing organizations to focus on their core business areas. With its suite of ICT Solutions, Cogeco Data Services provides its customers with flexible, end-to-end high availability solutions that are based on their IT needs, and backed by our reliable and timely 24x7x365 support services.

# DATA RECONCILIATION OFFERING GETS ITS CLIENTS ONBOARD WITH INTEGRATED VISUAL SOLUTION

The client has an integrated three-part solution that accurately reconciles large volumes of data quickly and allows mobile-secure access and provides precise distribution of confidential data to the correct audience. They had a significant happy client base for one of the solutions, but they did not understand that there were two other integrated parts to the solution. To make this fact obvious and intuitive, we came up with a digitized sketch of the three-step-integrated offering with a playful visual so everyone got it. The client liked the pencil sketches so much in the ideation process that they requested that the final render carry the same style.

**Content chaos contained**
Inconsistent, inaccurate data and unmanaged content ruining your day?

# VIDEO ANALYTICS FIRM DEMONSTRATES THE SOCIAL EFFECT OF SUPER BOWL ADS WITH DATA VISUALIZATION

Sometimes the best way to illustrate a ranked list is a ranked list. This particular data visualization allows the list to command the visual real estate space with some surround sound data points treated in the client's sophisticated brand design.

Super Bowl **Ad** Rankings
Earned Media

## Calculating Earned ROI of Super Bowl Ads

| | Advertisement | Earned Media* | Cumulative Viewership** |
|---|---|---|---|
| 1. | Honda CR-V 2012 - "Matthew's Day Off" | $2,243,275 | 14,762,276 |
| 2. | Acura NSX - "Transactions" | $2,175,464 | 18,534,151 |
| 3. | Chrysler - "Halftime in America" | $973,627 | 7,677,968 |
| 4. | VW "The Dog Strikes Back" | $754,369 | 9,471,291 |
| 5. | Fiat - "500 Abrath" | $490,451 | 7,428,379 |
| 6. | Audi - "Vampire Party" | $461,180 | 7,214,068 |
| 7. | Chevy Silverado "End of the World" | $450,587 | 6,934,674 |
| 8. | M&M'S - "Just My Shell" | $421,461 | 12,972,847 |
| 9. | Toyota Camry "It's Reinvented!" | $364,159 | 5,696,402 |
| 10. | Pepsi - "King's Court" | $285,833 | 4,471,186 |
| | Top 10 Cumulative: | $8,620,406 | 95,163,242 |
| | All Super Bowl Ads Cumulative | $11,114,526 | 148,636,444 |

The Super Bowl "Bounce"

**TOTAL VALUE CREATED**

| Pre-Game | Post-Game |
|---|---|
| $2,153,746 | $9,514,420 |

**TOTAL AD VIEWERSHIP**

| Pre-Game | Post-Game |
|---|---|
| 40,465,557 | 108,170,887 |

Social Recall Auto Ads***

| | Brand | Theme |
|---|---|---|
| 1. | Audi | 1. "Vampire" AUDI |
| 2. | Volkswagen | 2. "Dog" VOLKSWAGEN |
| 3. | Toyota | 3. "Jerry Seinfeld" ACURA |
| 4. | Acura | 4. "Ferris Bueller" HONDA |
| 5. | Honda | 5. "America" CHRYSLER |
| 6. | Chrysler | 6. "Reinvented" TOYOTA |

# SOCIAL MEDIA AND PR VISUAL SOLUTIONS

# ONLINE REAL ESTATE GETS ON *THE WALL STREET JOURNAL* BLOG

Just before the Halloween season, a client wanted to brainstorm how, through an infographic social media play, we could entertain its community and at the same time subtly suggest that the client knows a thing or two about real estate demographics. The result was a colorful and provocative infographic that leveraged proprietary data on city-specific real estate metrics to generate a list of the best cities to take children trick-or-treating. And it worked. *The Wall Street Journal* and other media outlets caught on to the list, and their communities started the city debate, while the client enjoyed a free brand lift around its online real estate data-backed knowledge.

# NEW NAME FOR CALIFORNIA CREDIT UNION CALLS FOR A NEW INFOGRAPHIC SOCIAL MEDIA PLAY

When a client decided to change its name and brand, it also made a proactive social media play to educate its community on the merits and conceptual differences between a bank and a credit union. As the infographic below shows, not all infographics have to be long and tall.

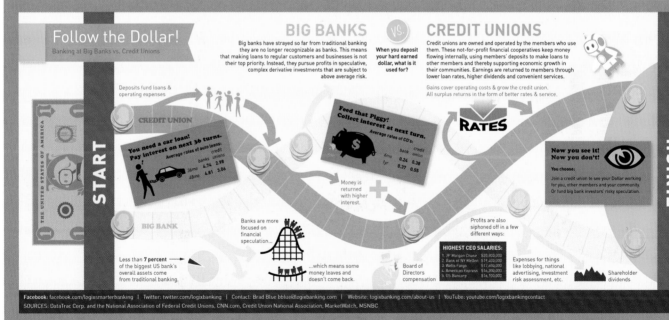

# RESEARCH VISUAL SOLUTIONS

- Enterprise Software Vendor Showcases Innovation with a Three-Part Infographic Series

- IT Hardware Provider Puts Viewer on Client Virtualization Journey

- Innovative Green Startup Showcases Energy Savings Research

# ENTERPRISE SOFTWARE VENDOR SHOWCASES INNOVATION WITH A THREE-PART INFOGRAPHIC SERIES

After a client commissioned custom research, they knew that the communication results could not simply show a technical feature list of their database solutions. Instead, they had to turn the "data" into a compelling and pressing topic of concern to any enterprise. This was all visualized in three lush infographic data stories on forecasting, innovation, and mobility.

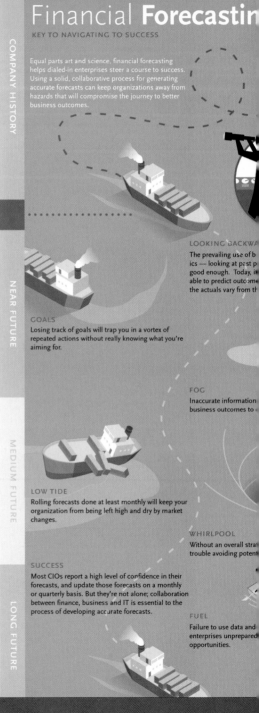

## Financial Forecastin

KEY TO NAVIGATING TO SUCCESS

Equal parts art and science, financial forecasting helps dialed-in enterprises steer a course to success. Using a solid, collaborative process for generating accurate forecasts can keep organizations away from hazards that will compromise the journey to better business outcomes.

COMPANY HISTORY

NEAR FUTURE

MEDIUM FUTURE

LONG FUTURE

LOOKING BACKWA
The prevailing use of b
ics — looking at past p
good enough. Today, it
able to predict outcome
the actuals vary from th

GOALS
Losing track of goals will trap you in a vortex of repeated actions without really knowing what you're aiming for.

FOG
Inaccurate information
business outcomes to

LOW TIDE
Rolling forecasts done at least monthly will keep your organization from being left high and dry by market changes.

WHIRLPOOL
Without an overall strat
trouble avoiding potent

SUCCESS
Most CIOs report a high level of confidence in their forecasts, and update those forecasts on a monthly or quarterly basis. But they're not alone; collaboration between finance, business and IT is essential to the process of developing accurate forecasts.

FUEL
Failure to use data and
enterprises unprepared
opportunities.

# The **Innovation Journey**

It's not the final destination, but the journey that matters most. Optimizing business and IT operations for innovation is a journey that passes through simplicity, speed, empowerment, insight and flexibility.

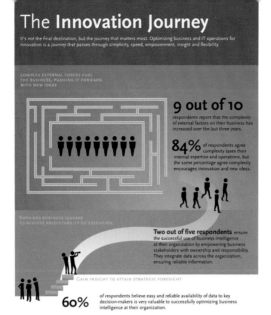

COMPLEX EXTERNAL FORCES FUEL THE BUSINESS, PUSHING IT FORWARD WITH NEW IDEAS

**9 out of 10**
respondents report that the complexity of external factors on their business has increased over the last three years.

**84%** of respondents agree complexity taxes their internal expertise and operations, but the same percentage agree complexity encourages innovation and new ideas.

EMPOWER BUSINESS LEADERS TO ACHIEVE PREDICTABILITY OF EXECUTION

**Two out of five respondents** ensure the successful use of business intelligence at their organization by empowering business stakeholders with ownership and responsibility. They integrate data across the organization, ensuring reliable information.

GAIN INSIGHT TO ATTAIN STRATEGIC FORESIGHT

**60%** of respondents believe easy and reliable availability of data to key decision-makers is very valuable to successfully optimizing business intelligence at their organization.

IT FLEXIBILITY BOOSTS ALIGNMENT, BRIDGES GOALS-EFFECTIVENESS GAP

Top IT priorities for organizations over the next year and a half include creating a flexible IT infrastructure and adapting or extending existing applications to support new technology initiatives.

But there's a big gap between goals and effectiveness: When we look at how important IT priorities are to organizations compared to how effective they are in these areas, we can easily find where the largest gaps are between value (importance of IT priorities) and performance (effectiveness of IT priorities). After performing a gap analysis, we found the largest gap between value and performance is in creating a flexible IT infrastructure, with a 42% difference between importance and effectiveness.

## Optimize operations to evolve from alignment to collaboration

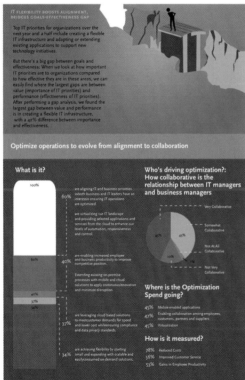

### What is it?

are aligning IT and business priorities: both business and IT leaders have an interest in ensuring IT operations are optimized.

are virtualizing our IT landscape and providing selected applications and services from the cloud to enhance our levels of automation, responsiveness and control.

are enabling increased employee and business productivity to improve competitive position.

Extending existing on-premise processes with mobile and cloud solutions to apply continuous innovation and minimize disruption.

are leveraging cloud-based solutions to meet customer demands for speed and lower cost while ensuring compliance and data privacy standards.

are achieving flexibility by starting small and expanding with scalable and easily consumed on-demand solutions.

### Who's driving optimization?: How collaborative is the relationship between IT managers and business managers

- Very Collaborative
- Somewhat Collaborative
- Not At All Collaborative
- Not Very Collaborative

### Where is the Optimization Spend going?

- 45% Mobile-enabled applications
- 47% Enabling collaboration among employees, customers, partners and suppliers
- 45% Virtualization

### How is it measured?

- 78% Reduced Costs
- 56% Improved Customer Service
- 53% Gains in Employee Productivity

This journey to optimization leads to innovation and successful outcomes
**LEARN MORE**

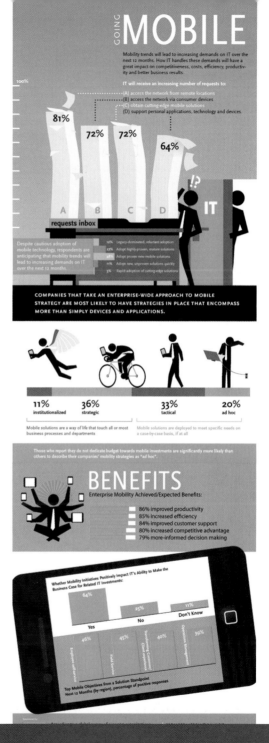

## GOING **MOBILE**

Mobility trends will lead to increasing demands on IT over the next 12 months. How IT handles these demands will have a great impact on competitiveness, costs, efficiency, productivity and better business results.

IT will receive an increasing number of requests to:
- (A) access the network from remote locations
- (B) access the network via consumer devices
- (C) obtain cutting-edge mobile solutions
- (D) support personal applications, technology and devices.

81% 72% 72% 64%
A B C D

requests inbox

Despite cautious adoption of mobile technology, respondents are anticipating that mobility trends will lead to increasing demands on IT over the next 12 months.
- 16% Legacy-dominated, reluctant adoption
- 27% Adopt highly-proven, mature solutions
- 38% Adopt proven new mobile solutions
- 11% Adopt new, unproven solutions quickly
- 3% Rapid adoption of cutting-edge solutions

**COMPANIES THAT TAKE AN ENTERPRISE-WIDE APPROACH TO MOBILE STRATEGY ARE MOST LIKELY TO HAVE STRATEGIES IN PLACE THAT ENCOMPASS MORE THAN SIMPLY DEVICES AND APPLICATIONS.**

**11%** institutionalized  **36%** strategic  **33%** tactical  **20%** ad hoc

Mobile solutions are a way of life that touch all or most business processes and departments

Mobile solutions are deployed to meet specific needs on a case-by-case basis, if at all

Those who report they do not dedicate budget towards mobile investments are significantly more likely than others to describe their companies' mobility strategies as "ad hoc".

## BENEFITS
Enterprise Mobility Achieved/Expected Benefits:

- 86% improved productivity
- 85% increased efficiency
- 84% improved customer support
- 80% increased competitive advantage
- 79% more-informed decision making

Whether Mobility Initiatives Positively Impact IT's Ability to Make the Business Case for Related IT Investments:

**64%** Yes  **25%** No  **11%** Don't Know

46%  45%  40%  39%

Top Mobile Objectives from a Solution Standpoint Next 12 Months (by region), percentage of positive responses

# IT HARDWARE PROVIDER PUTS VIEWER ON CLIENT VIRTUALIZATION JOURNEY

While the technical nuances and associated benefits can be better appreciated by a technical audience, the client wanted to widen to a broader audience. The research was designed into a fun, engaging road trip, allowing the data to tell its story every curve of the way.

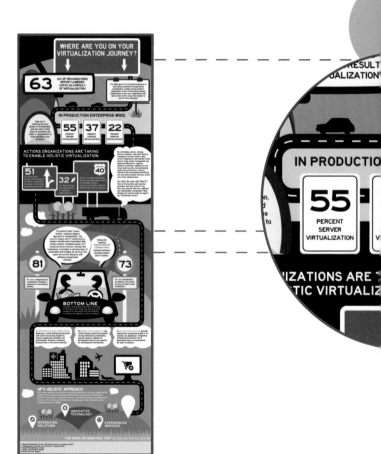

...anity-based health center ...d a virtual desktop infrastructure ...a back-end storage solution to ...prove application reliability and ...performance. Security is enhanced because data is now stored centrally.[5]

An online travel agency's... virtual storage system has double... storage utilization by eliminating unused capacity, enabling its development team to use capacity for development environments.

## HP'S HOLISTIC APPROACH

HP's holistic approach to virtualization can help organizations like yours realize the full potential of this enabling technology. With the most comprehensive virtualization ...ortfolio in the industry—integrated solutions, innovative technology, and experienced ...ices—HP can help you transform your business by turning virtualization into a ...ic business advantage.

...to take a more ...usiness-aligned ...o virtualization. The ...s with IT establishing a ...astructure foundation that ...ared, virtualized pools of IT ...s across servers, storage and ...g. It includes a common layer of ...ation that bridges all services and spans the service lifecycle with unifying management software.

Doing this requires **unprecedented collaboration** between business decision makers and IT leaders.

**TERPRISE-WI...**

7 | 22
PERCENT DESKTOP VIRTUALIZATION[2]

INNOVATIVE
TECHNO...

...1% say a comprehensive ...irtualization strategy is ...mportant to maximizing ...enefits.

73

73% say virtualization investments are paving the way for future cloud enablement.[4]

...G
N:

By virtualizing s... devices, netwo... companies c... array of i... time to... impr...

40

## BOTTOM LINE
A modern, end-to-end converged virtualized infrastructure will make your business more competitive, more agile, and more attuned to meeting the demands of your customers.

...ter

An online travel a...

# INNOVATIVE GREEN STARTUP SHOWCASES ENERGY SAVINGS RESEARCH

A startup did its research and came to the interesting conclusion that the leading energy waster in large corporate buildings was, in fact, lighting. They came up with an innovative motion detection and software solution that reduced lighting based on real-time occupancy and showed a significant reduction in energy costs. This visualization explained how the solution worked, with an interesting and relevant building cutaway, and then showed the energy savings in dynamic data visualizations.

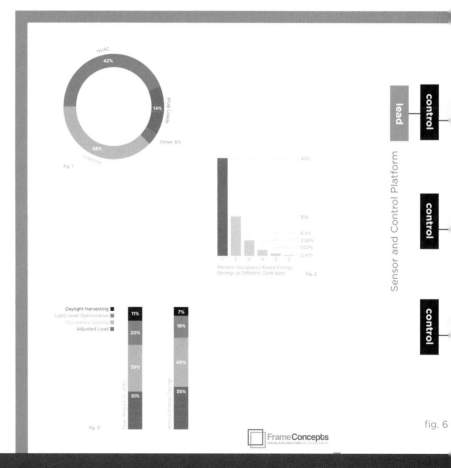

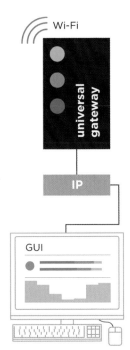

Wi-Fi

universal gateway

Building Network

IP

GUI

Maintenence and
Management Portal

sensor

sensor

sensor

# SALES AND MARKETING VISUAL SOLUTIONS

- Leading Reputation Consultancy Markets Their Insight Workshop

- Social Media Recruitment Platform Visualizes Steps in Sales

- New Product Release in the Enterprise Risk Space Gets a Visual Product Brochure

# LEADING REPUTATION CONSULTANCY MARKETS THEIR INSIGHT WORKSHOP

This client can provide data-fed intelligence on social channel content impact not only on reputation but on how it ties to your bottom line if remedial action is not taken. We created a clever tabbed visual invite to the workshop to underscore the importance of attending, and then came up with a clever client slide presentation that, through data visualization, drove the point home on their recommendations.

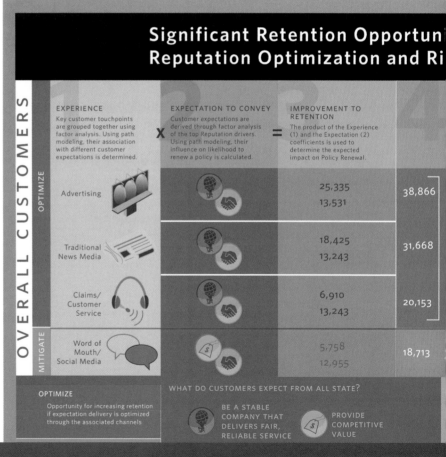

## from
## Mitigation

**OVERALL REPUTATION
IMPACT ON RETENTION**

Impact of Reputation in terms
of Net New Policy Renewals
(Customers) is determined using
assumptions outlined below.

ONAL BENEFIT
IMIZATION
7

**109,399**
RETAINED CUSTOMERS

Key Assumptions:
Retention Rate = 87.9%
Protection Households = 11,896,417

TS OF
TION

UTATION RETENTION THRESHOLDS
OVERALL CUSTOMERS

**83.9** VERY WILLING TO
BUY NEW POLICY

# WHERE WE ARE
# TODAY

Our research has sought to identify
these gaps in Fidelity's communications
strategy and understand the
perception-altering challenges facing
the **seven key stakeholder groups.**

With this information, we can sythesize
an accurate simulation of the stakeholder ecosystem.

policy makers

workplace

personal

employees

institutional

media

opinion-makers

Where We Are Today

Where We'll Be Tomorrow

What We Need From You

The Simulation Itself

**SALES AND MARKETING VISUAL SOLUTIONS**

203

# SOCIAL MEDIA RECRUITMENT PLATFORM VISUALIZES STEPS IN SALES

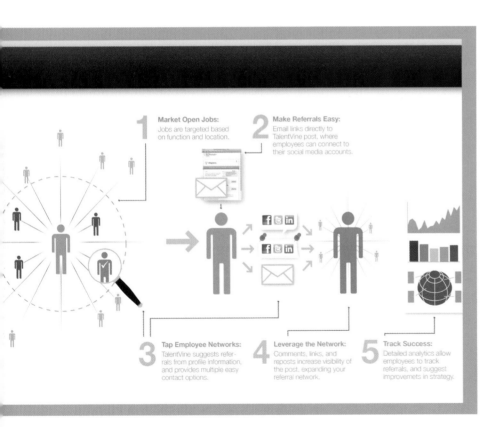

**Market Open Jobs:**
1 Jobs are targeted based on function and location.

**Make Referrals Easy:**
2 Email links directly to TalentVine post, where employees can connect to their social media accounts.

**Tap Employee Networks:**
3 TalentVine suggests referrals from profile information, and provides multiple easy contact options.

**Leverage the Network:**
4 Comments, links, and reposts increase visibility of the post, expanding your referral network.

**Track Success:**
5 Detailed analytics allow employees to track referrals, and suggest improvemets in strategy.

A clever idea to tie employees' social networks to the referral programs of the HR department needed some visual explanatory support. The client wanted to take the audience through the steps of their unique offering with a staged sales presentation. The marketing department was also concerned that the visuals were sophisticated and showed a keen sense of modern design. Through a unique blend of modern colors and typography and limiting the illustration palette to only iconic designs, a fresh and persuasive infographic sales deck was created.

# NEW PRODUCT RELEASE IN THE ENTERPRISE RISK SPACE GETS A VISUAL PRODUCT BROCHURE

The client was very excited about an upcoming release by which their risk clients now could download and develop applications and extensions with only a business user's knowledge, much like the consumer could download an application on their i-Phone or iPad. To visually seize on that excitement, we came up with an innovative product brochure that leverages the smartphone app space metaphor to drive the point home.

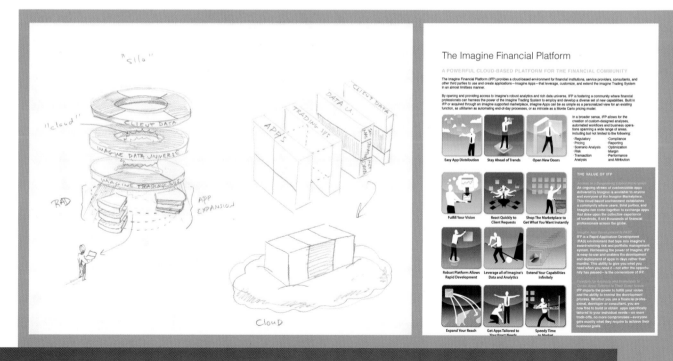

# PRODUCT DEVELOPMENT AND PROGRAMMERS

- Nuclear Spare Parts Provider Wanted to Dynamically Visualize Spare Parts

- Pension Fund: Security Impact on Bottom Line

- Innovative Media Analytics Platform Unifies Online Television Metrics on One Dashboard

# NUCLEAR SPARE PARTS PROVIDER WANTED TO DYNAMICALLY VISUALIZE SPARE PARTS

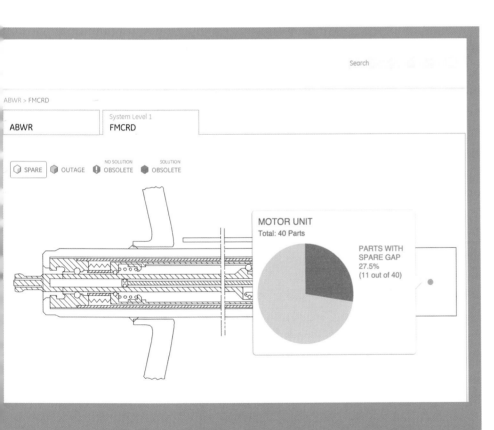

There are not a lot of new nuclear reactors being built, but there are legacy reactors that require spare parts to be stocked and replacement parts for obsolete items to be engineered. However, the nuclear reactor clients were forced to go through reams and reams of spreadsheets to determine what the status of each part actually was. So we developed a prototype to visualize spare parts status for both the nuclear reactor and the control room. The key was a red pulsating point that dynamically allowed the client to navigate quickly to the spare part of concern and see a visual of the actual part in question and its status.

# PENSION FUND: SECURITY IMPACT ON BOTTOM LINE

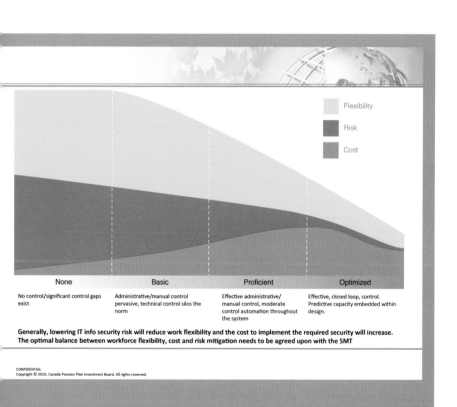

With new ideas around innovative security technologies and protocol affecting IT budgets, line of business flexibility, and the amount of security breaches, the client wanted a dashboard that would visualize the relationships among security measures, costs, business flexibility, and security breaches. A key visual was developed to win over each line of business to the right balance between cost, business flexibility, and security.

# INNOVATIVE MEDIA ANALYTICS PLATFORM UNIFIES ONLINE TELEVISION METRICS ON ONE DASHBOARD

The thought of unifying advertising metrics on both online and television channels all in one platform was so innovative that the client requested an interface prototype with intuitive data visualization to show their beta clients the reality of what they were proposing.

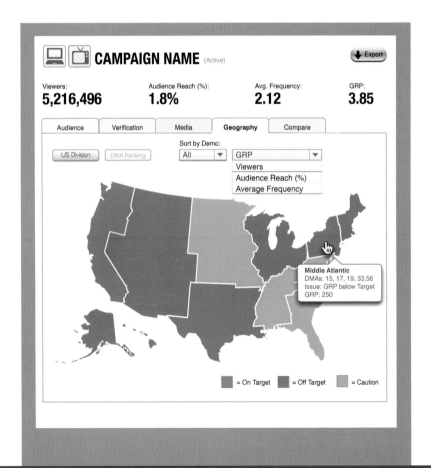

# CONSTRUCTION AND REAL ESTATE INDUSTRY VISUAL SOLUTIONS

- Showcasing an Innovative Construction Solution on a Tablet

- Green Energy Startup Showcases Approach and Savings with Infographic

- Real Estate Infographic Goes *Wall Street Journal* Viral

# SHOWCASING AN INNOVATIVE CONSTRUCTION SOLUTION ON A TABLET

The client had developed an innovative approach to providing real-time updates on construction status for large construction projects for all players, including field teams, management, facilities operations, architects, and business owners. To highlight that, they could be viewed in the field on a tablet. An interactive "before" and "after" pictogram that displayed on a tablet itself was developed.

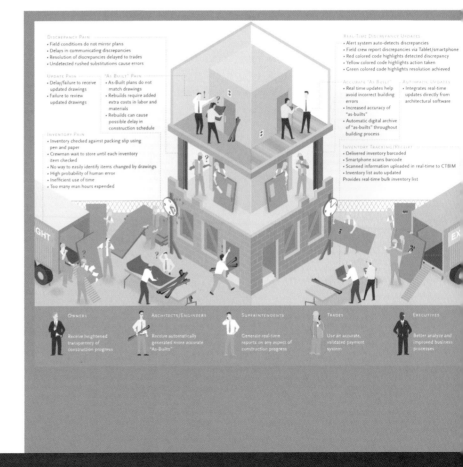

# GREEN ENERGY STARTUP SHOWCASES APPROACH AND SAVINGS WITH INFOGRAPHIC

A false sense of complacency with valuable possessions in the home was shaken with this provocative infographic based on actual housing break-in crime statistics. While the actual solution lurking behind the infographic was a physical safe, the infographic was effective in bring the need for the solution to the forefront for the homeowner.

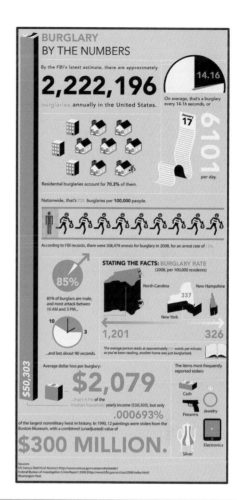

## Outline Ideas

1. How about does a break-in look like – average value, popular items, where they break in.
   Favorite items include: cash, jewelry, laptops, guns, digital cameras, small electronics (Ipods, GPS, PDA's MP-3's and CD's). Money is usually used to support a drug habit. Breakin typically takes 60 seconds or less.
2. When do most break-in occur?
   Usually occur in the daytime when occupants are at school or work.
   July and August most the frequent months for break-ins.
   February is the least frequent for home breaks.
3. How are homes targeted?
   Simple selection process
   Choose an unoccupied home with easy access, the greatest amount of cover and the best escape routes.
   Homeowners often make this selection process easy for thieves by failing to take simple precautions.

# REAL ESTATE INFOGRAPHIC GOES *WALL STREET JOURNAL* VIRAL

This infographic was a clever way to balance the art of offering entertaining content with a subtle suggestion that the client knows a lot about national housing marketplace metrics. The client is one of the largest online real estate platforms in the world. It achieved this for Halloween season by showcasing the best trick-or-treating cities by compiling relevant housing metrics. This provocative infographic caught the attention of *The Wall Street Journal,* where bloggers pushed the message virally by further debating the actual list.

## Trick-or-Treat In

The data geeks and candy lovers at Z
mathematical approach to ranking th
or-treat across the country. Where do

### 20 Best Cities to Trick-or-Treat

1. San Francisco
2. Boston
3. Honolulu
4. Seattle
5. Chicago
6. San Jose
7. Washington
8. Los Angeles
9. Philadelphia
10. Portland
11. Minneapolis
12. Pittsburgh
13. San Diego
14. Cleveland
15. Miami
16. Denver
17. Milwaukee
18. Virginia Beach
19. Baltimore
20. Albuquerque

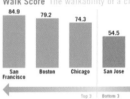

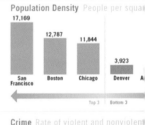

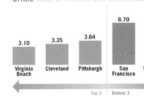

Methodology: The third annual Zillow Trick-or-Treat Index was c
equally weighted data variables and represents cities that will p
candy, with the least walking and safety risks.

: 2011

ave taken a
cities to trick-
city stack up?

lex

$50,514
Cleveland

40.8
Virginia
Beach

1,759
Virginia
Beach

7.89

Miami

using four
the most

## The Best Cities For Trick-Or-Treating

| Article | Comments (24) |
| --- | --- |

There are 24 Comment(s)

Go to most recent | Add a Comment
To report offensive comments email thejuggle@wsj.com

Sort by:  Oldest | Newest

1:51 pm October 20, 2011

**North of Boston** wrote:

I still have very fond memories of the night (about 30 years ago) when I went trick-or-treating with friends on Beacon Hill in Boston. For me, that was the ultimate. Our current north-of-Boston town is good, too — the streets are densely populated, but also quiet and safe, so we get a lot of trick-or-treaters. People even drive in from neighboring towns to trick-or-treat in our area. It's a really fun, festive atmosphere on Halloween night.

1:54 pm October 20, 2011

**ratgirlny** wrote:

We get a LOT of trick or treaters in our neighborhood. We have pretty close together houses and sidewalks, which I think is a big factor. My kids really look forward to Halloween.

2:30 pm October 20, 2011

**Charlotte Juggler** wrote:

Charlotte has big housing developments so I think most suburban kids trick or treat within their immediate neighborhood. Our neighborhood is a mix of age ranges so the number of kids is limited.

In our old Boston neighborhood we got tons of trick or treaters from different surrounding streets. We were also close to a middle school so we tended to get older kids. Trick or treating tended to go on till much later.

2:36 pm October 20, 2011

**Honolulu mother** wrote:

We don't get a whole lot of trick-or-treaters at our house since we're on a busier road, but about five minutes' walk from our house is the beginning of a network of non-artery neighborhood streets that is always packed with trick-or-treaters. So we trick-or-treat our way down to that part of the neighborhood.

# EDUCATION INDUSTRY VISUAL SOLUTIONS

# VISUAL ENGAGEMENT FOR LITERACY LEARNING APPLICATION

The client believes that technology can be a key differentiator to help bridge the literacy gap in the American school system. This was storyboarded as a fun but core curriculum-packed lesson to up the engagement and learning factors. Seen here are some of the concept sketches that are a crucial part of the application development process.

# TABLET VENDOR SHOWS HOW TABLETS ARE THE NEXT GENERATION CLASSROOM

This colorful and engaging info-graphic showcases how tablets can increase the interactive learning experience in today's classrooms. Instead of leveraging a conceptual analogy, the tablets are placed in the classroom context to drive the point home that it is not a concept, but reality that can be engaged with now.

## TABLETS ARE AT THE FOREFRONT OF THE NEXT-GENERATION CLASSROOM

58%

Of kids aged 13 to 17 have a smart phone

31%

In grades 6-8 use tablets for homework

Rapid advances in the technology industry are bringing new opportunities for schools and teachers to find innovative tools to enhance student education.

School districts are responding, and now a majority are looking at providing tablets to students rather than traditional desktops and notebooks.

### FROM PASSIVE TO PARTICIPATORY

### NEW TABLET DEVICES AND SOFTWARE ENABLE THIS COLLABORATION BY PROVIDING

### THE EVOLUTION OF THE INTERACTIVE CLASSROOM

Educational applications and digital content such as digital textbooks

SCHOOL

SAMSUNG SCHOOL

---

## CLASSROOM

Rapid advances in the technology industry are bringing new opportunities for schools and teachers to find innovative tools to enhance student education.

Today's tech-savvy K-12 pupils have grown up with electronic devices. They're "digital natives." As a result, they're more responsive to technology and better engaged in the learning experience when these tools are part of their classroom environment.

31%

In grades 6-8 us tablets for homew

districts are and now a king at

# HIGHER EDUCATION GETS AN ROI VISUALIZATION

The client had come up with a revolutionary tool to leverage an enterprise software approach for the administration of college athletic departments to improve efficiencies and savings. The following slide leverages iconography and data visualization to showcase on one slide the amount and categories of savings that college athletic departments could enjoy if they employ the solution.

## Saves Duke Athletics Thousands

 time savings   monetized time savings   hard goods savings

 electronic forms

| | | |
|---|---|---|
| 🕐 | 2,727.04 hrs | = 54.54 hrs/week 10.9 hrs/day |
| | $73,521.00 | 16,441 TOTAL ASSIGNMENTS |
| | $1,713.46 | 44,390 TOTAL PAGES SAVED |
| TOTAL | $75,234.46 | |

metrics

| | | |
|---|---|---|
| 🕐 | 91.59 hrs | = 1.83 hrs/week 0.4 hrs/day |
| | $2,164.27 | 29 |
| TOTAL | $2,164.27 | TOTAL METRIC TYPES |

 file sharing

| | | |
|---|---|---|
| 🕐 | 77.23 hrs | = 1.54 hrs/week 0.3 hrs/day |
| | $2,082.12 | 53,572 PAGES SAVED |
| | $1,179.26 | |

orks tools create time and hard goods cost savings for teams, athletic departments, and conferences the country. As the only platform focused on increasing internal efficiency, Teamworks is the premier r of the tools your department needs to cut costs and save staff time.

niversity Athletics invested in Teamworks to streamline internal operations, improve communications, ize data, and increase collaboration. The Teamworks platform solution saves Duke Athletics an annual f $244,304.72.

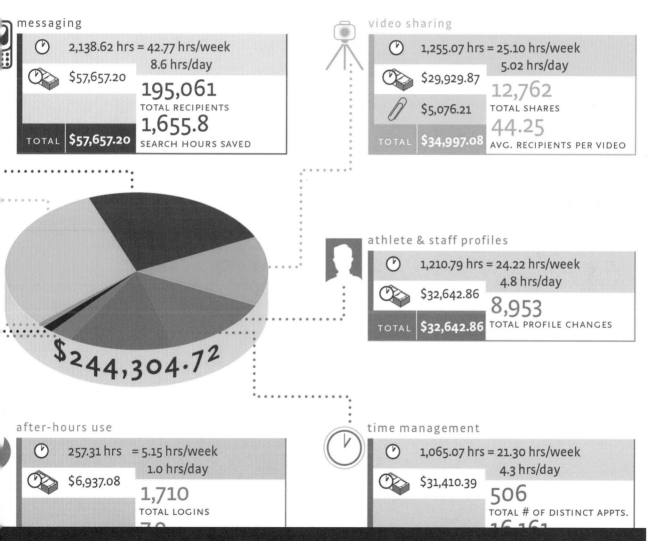

### messaging

| 🕐 | 2,138.62 hrs = 42.77 hrs/week |
| | 8.6 hrs/day |
| 💰 | $57,657.20 |
| | **195,061** |
| | TOTAL RECIPIENTS |
| | **1,655.8** |
| TOTAL **$57,657.20** | SEARCH HOURS SAVED |

### video sharing

| 🕐 | 1,255.07 hrs = 25.10 hrs/week |
| | 5.02 hrs/day |
| 💰 | $29,929.87 |
| | **12,762** |
| 📎 | $5,076.21 |
| | TOTAL SHARES |
| | **44.25** |
| TOTAL **$34,997.08** | AVG. RECIPIENTS PER VIDEO |

### athlete & staff profiles

| 🕐 | 1,210.79 hrs = 24.22 hrs/week |
| | 4.8 hrs/day |
| 💰 | $32,642.86 |
| | **8,953** |
| TOTAL **$32,642.86** | TOTAL PROFILE CHANGES |

### after-hours use

| 🕐 | 257.31 hrs = 5.15 hrs/week |
| | 1.0 hrs/day |
| 💰 | $6,937.08 |
| | **1,710** |
| | TOTAL LOGINS |

### time management

| 🕐 | 1,065.07 hrs = 21.30 hrs/week |
| | 4.3 hrs/day |
| 💰 | $31,410.39 |
| | **506** |
| | TOTAL # OF DISTINCT APPTS. |

# ENERGY INDUSTRY VISUAL SOLUTIONS

- Dynamically Displaying Spare Parts Status

- Green Energy Startup Showcases Approach and Savings with Infographic

- Dynamically Displaying the Control Room in 3D

# DYNAMICALLY DISPLAYING SPARE PARTS STATUS

While construction of new nuclear reactors has slowed down, the management and supply of spare parts for legacy reactors is a fertile business. To enable its clients to quickly see what parts need to be ordered, we created a dynamic data-fed visualization of quantity and obsolescence status of spare parts. Instead of poring through reams and reams of spreadsheets, red pulsating spots dynamically displayed where their clients need to focus their attention.

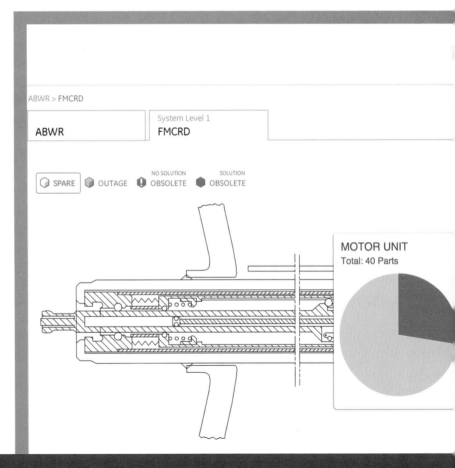

ABWR > FMCRD

ABWR

System Level 1
FMCRD

SPARE · OUTAGE · NO SOLUTION OBSOLETE · SOLUTION OBSOLETE

MOTOR UNIT
Total: 40 Parts

# GREEN ENERGY STARTUP SHOWCASES APPROACH AND SAVINGS WITH INFOGRAPHIC

A California-based green energy startup developed technology and an approach that delivered the most energy savings with the largest energy category for large office buildings—lighting. This infographic shows how the sensors coupled to computing programs delivered the solution, while a colorful dynamic visualization showcased the actual savings.

fig. 6

# DYNAMICALLY DISPLAYING THE CONTROL ROOM IN 3D

We had already provided the prototype for the dynamic visualization of spare parts status within the nuclear reactor; now the project turned to the control room that controlled the reactor. Because the electronics sat in racks on an angle to the controller staff, a visual decision was made to simulate the 3D aspect of the control room. The net effect was to make the entire application more engaging and intuitive.

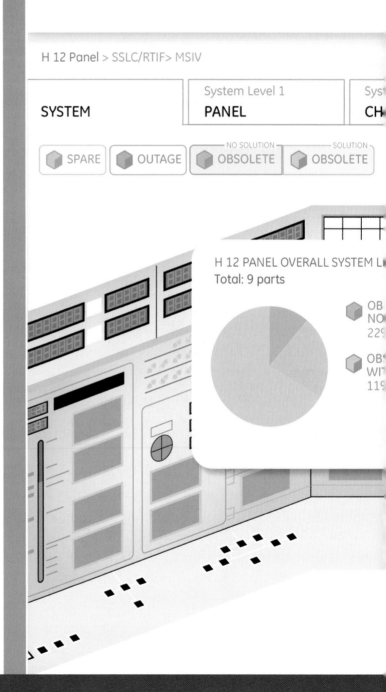

vel 2

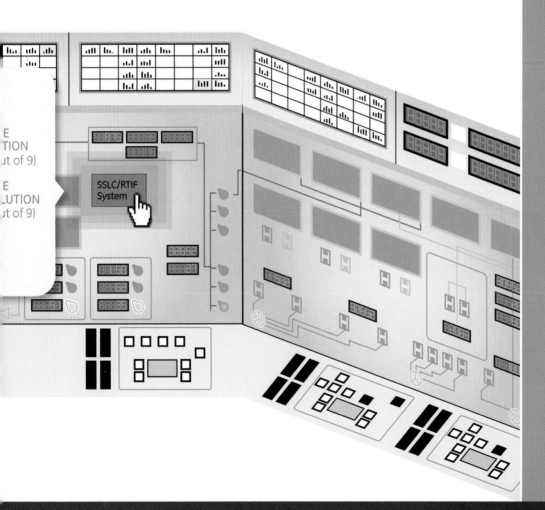

E
TION
ut of 9)

E
UTION
ut of 9)

SSLC/RTIF
System

# FINANCIAL SERVICES VISUAL SOLUTIONS

- Showcases New Trading Communication Platform

- Credit Union Drives Distinction Between a Bank and a Credit Union

- Insurance Brokers Association Showcases Their Membership in Numbers

# SHOWCASES NEW TRADING COMMUNICATION PLATFORM

The client wanted to showcase how their new Trading Communication Platform provided value to the front, middle, and back office, as well as for the IT team. We developed an engaging pictogram that showed the audience in a figurative "trading platform" and also introduced the value points with interactive buttons that drove sequences and callouts that linked to further technical documentation about the offering.

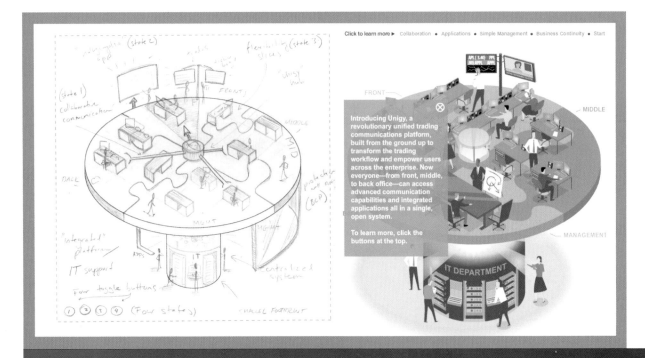

# CREDIT UNION DRIVES DISTINCTION BETWEEN A BANK AND A CREDIT UNION

Off of a launch of new company name and brand, the client wanted to clear the slate so their customers could appreciate the benefits of joining a credit union over a bank. This journey through a game board made conceptual distinctions easy to digest.

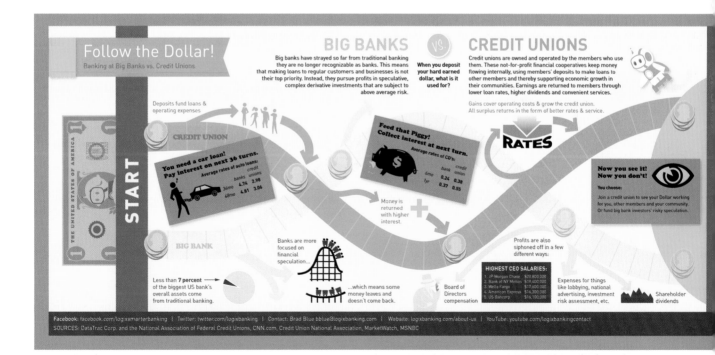

**Follow the Dollar!**
Banking at Big Banks vs. Credit Unions

## BIG BANKS

Big banks have strayed so far from traditional banking they are no longer recognizable as banks. This means that making loans to regular customers and businesses is not their top priority. Instead, they pursue profits in speculative, complex derivative investments that are subject to above average risk.

When you deposit your hard earned dollar, what is it used for?

## CREDIT UNIONS

Credit unions are owned and operated by the members who use them. These not-for-profit financial cooperatives keep money flowing internally, using members' deposits to make loans to other members and thereby supporting economic growth in their communities. Earnings are returned to members through lower loan rates, higher dividends and convenient services.

Gains cover operating costs & grow the credit union.
All surplus returns in the form of better rates & service.

Deposits fund loans & operating expenses

**CREDIT UNION**

**START**

**You need a car loan! Pay interest on next 36 turns.**
Average rates of auto loans:

|  | banks | credit unions |
|---|---|---|
| 36mo | 4.74 | 2.98 |
| 48mo | 4.81 | 3.06 |

**Feed that Piggy! Collect interest at next turn.**
Average rates of CD's:

|  | bank | credit union |
|---|---|---|
| 6mo | 0.24 | 0.38 |
| 1yr | 0.37 | 0.55 |

**RATES**

**Now you see it! Now you don't!**
You choose:
Join a credit union to see your Dollar working for you, other members and your community. Or fund big bank investors' risky speculation.

Money is returned with higher interest.

**BIG BANK**

Less than **7 percent** of the biggest US bank's overall assets come from traditional banking.

Banks are more focused on financial speculation...

...which means some money leaves and doesn't come back.

Board of Directors compensation

Profits are also siphoned off in a few different ways:

**HIGHEST CEO SALARIES:**
1. JP Morgan Chase  $20,800,000
2. Bank of NY Mellon  $19,400,000
3. Wells Fargo  $17,600,000
4. American Express  $14,300,000
5. US Bancorp  $16,100,000

Expenses for things like lobbying, national advertising, investment risk assessment, etc.

Shareholder dividends

Facebook: facebook.com/logixsmarterbanking  |  Twitter: twitter.com/logixbanking  |  Contact: Brad Blue bblue@logixbanking.com  |  Website: logixbanking.com/about-us  |  YouTube: youtube.com/logixbankingcontact
SOURCES: DataTrac Corp. and the National Association of Federal Credit Unions, CNN.com, Credit Union National Association, MarketWatch, MSNBC

# INSURANCE BROKERS ASSOCIATION SHOWCASES THEIR MEMBERSHIP IN NUMBERS

The client wanted to showcase the impressive things they had been doing for their members. The good thing was that everything was quantifiable, so rather that hide this fact with illustrations, in this case we let the numbers be the star of the show with some clever use of iconography and an information-design-based narrative to make the number journey engaging.

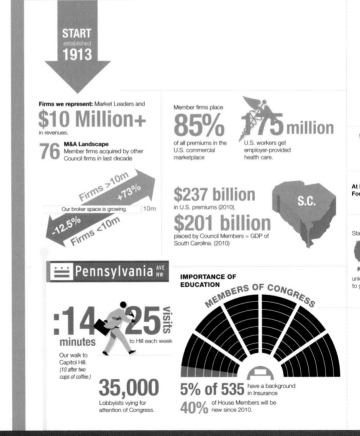

**START**
established
**1913**

**Firms we represent:** Market Leaders and
**$10 Million+**
in revenues.

**76** **M&A Landscape**
Member firms acquired by other
Council firms in last decade

Firms >10m
+73%
Our broker space is growing. | 10m
-12.5%
Firms <10m

Member firms place
**85%**
of all premiums in the
U.S. commercial
marketplace

**175 million**
U.S. workers get
employer-provided
health care.

**$237 billion**
in U.S. premiums (2010).
**$201 billion**
placed by Council Members = GDP of
South Carolina. (2010)

S.C.

**Pennsylvania** AVE NW

**:14 minutes**
Our walk to
Capitol Hill.
*(10 after two
cups of coffee.)*

**25 visits**
to Hill each week

**35,000**
Lobbyists vying for
attention of Congress.

**IMPORTANCE OF
EDUCATION**
MEMBERS OF CONGRESS

**5% of 535** have a background
in Insurance
**40%** of House Members will be
new since 2010.

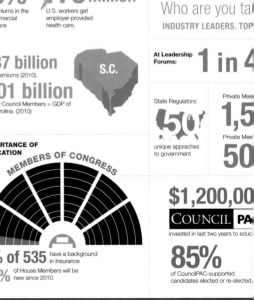

1 ILF App.
**37,000**
Pageviews.

Who are you ta
**INDUSTRY LEADERS. TOP**

**At Leadership
Forums:** **1 in 4**

State Regulators:
**50**
unique appraches
to government

Private Mee
**1,5**

Private Mee
**50**

**$1,200,00**
**COUNCIL PA**
invested in last two years to educ

**85%**
of CouncilPAC-supported
candidates elected or re-elected.

**Access to network**
members in

**128**
countries,

**4915**
offices worldwide

Only 1 broker-focused
magazine: Leader's Edge

**28**
awards for excellence

@#?*!

22 *Uncommon-tary* videos.
1 blooper reel *(and it's in a vault)*

FAME **133**
Scholarships, $665,000
Investing in the future.

**Bold Ideas.**
**TAKE**:20
Reflect. Reset.

to? Who are you listening to?
MS. FULL SPECTRUM OF THE MARKET PRESENT.

Council Market Surveys
cited in Moody's,
Bloomberg, Dow Jones,
Wall Street Journal,
industry trades and more.

**4,598**
Tweets in 2012
2,216 Followers
1,000+ RTs

**SMART RESOURCES =
HEALTHY FIRMS**
• Attract, retain & grow top talent
• Council Compensation Survey
• Pre-Employment Assessments
• Working Groups
• Leadership Workshops

es are
nts.

**TIME SAVED IS
MONEY EARNED:**

**4** days
per
Forum

**× 5** meetings
per day

**20** mtgs.

**$500** ✈
**$250** ◆
**+ $150** 🔧

**× $900** avg.
cost per
trip

= **$18,000**
saved by attending Council Forums

**Legal Time Spent:**
health care reform + surplus lines + compliance surveys =

**965hrs/24=125 days
or $386,000**

**1**

VOICE.
NETWORK.
RESOURCE.

**24+ years**
Joel Wood – a respected and consistent
voice for commercial brokerage industry

**90%/10%**
defense.     offense
**LASER-FOCUSED ADVOCACY.**

# VISUAL SOLUTIONS FOR THE HEALTHCARE INDUSTRY

- New Community-Based Delivery Model Gets Visual

- Offering Interactive Training Game to Showcase Managed Services

- Dental Kits Distribution Visualization

# NEW COMMUNITY-BASED DELIVERY MODEL GETS VISUAL

Instead of waiting for incoming patients at the hospital, the client came up with a new paradigm whereby they would proactively reach out and educate people within the community using the latest technologies. This paradigm shift will lower healthcare costs and increase overall wellness within the community by preventing the problem before it becomes a emergency room situation. The following pictogram showcases the model and shows the value it has for all stakeholders.

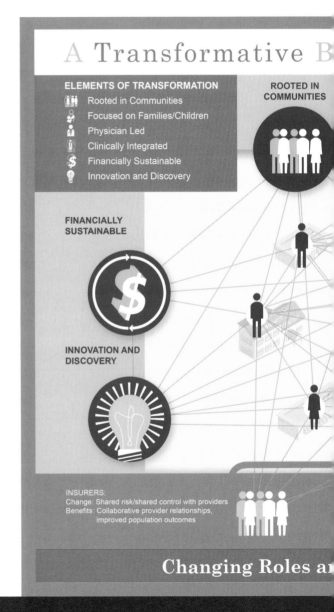

# siness Model for Pediatric Health

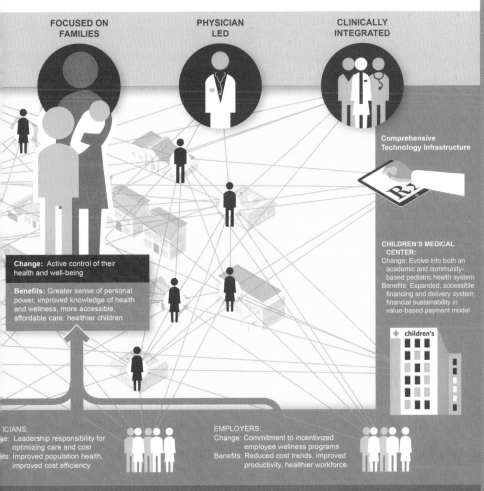

**FOCUSED ON FAMILIES**

**PHYSICIAN LED**

**CLINICALLY INTEGRATED**

Comprehensive Technology Infrastructure

**Change:** Active control of their health and well-being

**Benefits:** Greater sense of personal power, improved knowledge of health and wellness, more accessible, affordable care: healthier children

**CHILDREN'S MEDICAL CENTER:**
Change: Evolve into both an academic and community-based pediatric health system
Benefits: Expanded, accessible financing and delivery system; financial sustainability in value-based payment model

children's

ICIANS:
e: Leadership responsibility for optimizing care and cost
ts: Improved population health, improved cost efficiency

EMPLOYERS:
Change: Commitment to incentivized employee wellness programs
Benefits: Reduced cost trends, improved productivity, healthier workforce

# Responsibilities for Key Stakeholders

# OFFERING INTERACTIVE TRAINING GAME TO SHOWCASE MANAGED SERVICES

When management decided to reorder their approach to their managed services, they wanted to incorporate the feedback of staff, so created an interactive card training game in which the class gets to discuss the right order and approach while manipulating the service cards. The training tool delivered both on engagement and improvement feedback from those on the front line.

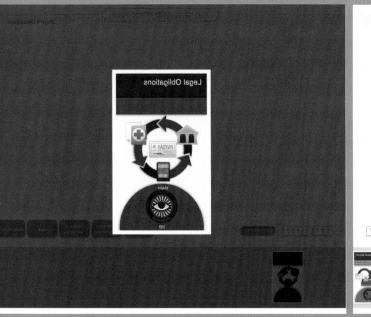

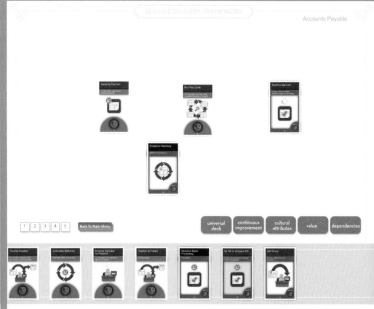

# DENTAL KITS DISTRIBUTION VISUALIZATION

Underprivileged children were not getting the appropriate dental care. The charity-based client was making an impact on delivering them into the right hands through the school system. The slide visualization made use of iconography to show impact as well as attract more donations to expand the program.

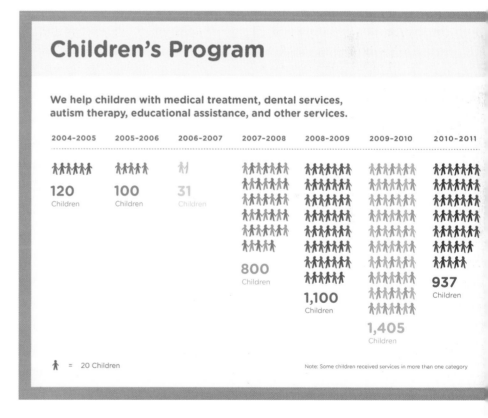

## Children's Program

**We help children with medical treatment, dental services, autism therapy, educational assistance, and other services.**

| 2004-2005 | 2005-2006 | 2006-2007 | 2007-2008 | 2008-2009 | 2009-2010 | 2010-2011 |
|---|---|---|---|---|---|---|
| 120 Children | 100 Children | 31 Children | 800 Children | 1,100 Children | 1,405 Children | 937 Children |

= 20 Children

Note: Some children received services in more than one category

# HR AND RECRUITING INDUSTRY VISUAL SOLUTIONS

- Social and Mobile Recruiting Solution Gets Interactive and Visual

- Social Employee Referral Program Gets a Visual Sales Slide Presentation

- Pharmaceutical Merger Visually Translated into Improved Employee Experience

# SOCIAL AND MOBILE RECRUITING SOLUTION GETS INTERACTIVE AND VISUAL

The client augmented its leading job board distribution system with a social recruiting solution. This pictogram shows that the solution augments the job board distribution system by adding candidates from social and mobile channels and reporting on all channels with an integrated analytics solution. This pictogram offered animated and interactive engagement for online distribution.

It's easy! eQuest sets up everything—log in, pick your jobs, click, you're done!

MIX distributes your job opportunities to a vast, new, relevant audience that shares the message, providing free, viral exposure to their personal friends, family and business colleagues.

MIX automatica jobs on Facebo LinkedIn and ar popular social d meets your crite

# The New World of Recruiting

Social Networks and Mobile devices have changed recruiting forever. To grab attention, you need to get the right message to the right people at the right time. eQuest and OptiJob formed "MIX" by combining a world-class job distribution platform with a cutting-edge Social and Mobile Media marketing platform to give eQuest clients a one-of-a-kind viral job marketing distribution solution. MIX seamlessly posts jobs across any Social Network, Community, Blog and Affinity Group that meets a client's recruiting goals.

MIX is an enterprise-level, hosted software solution that continuously streams and monitors thousands of jobs to a limitless number of social networks in real-time. To post a job, you just point and click—that's it! Jobs are automatically formatted and distributed to the specifications of each destination, and appended with unique tracking codes to monitor performance.

eQuest is the same proven distribution partner you have always trusted and OptiJob is the same proven partner that we have always trusted.

Global reach job board

Talent analytics platform

Social talent analytics stream

Viral exposure

Social talent

Does it work? Easily track response and campaign performance to ensure a positive ROI.

Quickly increase your talent audience and applicant pool with MIX.

# SOCIAL EMPLOYEE REFERRAL PROGRAM GETS A VISUAL SALES SLIDE PRESENTATION

The client had come up with a clever way to tie company's employee referral program into employees' social networks. The sales team needed a way to present the process, and clever use of iconography produced clear and engaging sales slides.

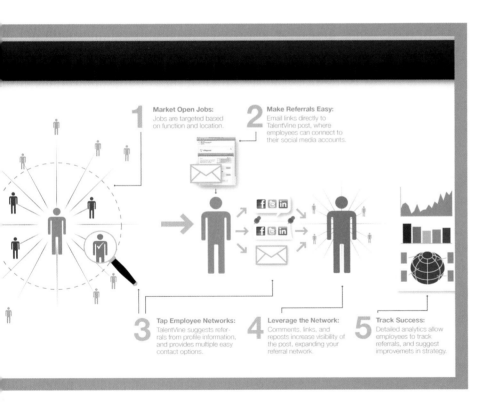

# PHARMACEUTICAL MERGER VISUALLY TRANSLATED INTO IMPROVED EMPLOYEE EXPERIENCE

When a client was going through a large merger, their HR department produced a pictogram to showcase the numerous benefits for employees on both sides of the merger.

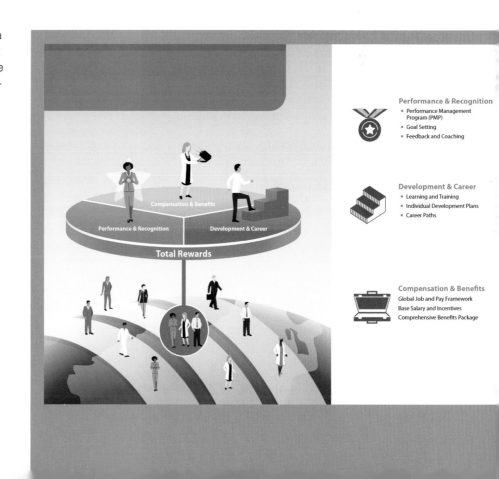

# IDEATION AND PRODUCT DEVELOPMENT INDUSTRY VISUAL SOLUTIONS

- Finance New Credit Approval Process: Storyboarding Ideation Phase

- Innovation Lab Rolling Out New Financial Data-Driven Solutions

- Collaborative Tool Goes Through Visual Ideation Phase

# FINANCE NEW CREDIT APPROVAL PROCESS: STORYBOARDING IDEATION PHASE

A client wanted to make the credit approval process with consumers in big box retailers more transparent and easy to follow. We supported the ideation process and client buy-in by storyboarding use cases for each alternative idea in context.

# INNOVATION LAB ROLLING OUT NEW FINANCIAL DATA-DRIVEN SOLUTIONS

This client has long cornered the market on business ratings with the ubiquitous risk number. The question became how they could roll out more profitable offerings while keeping true to their unique financial data roots. The idea, as shown in these initial ideation sketches, was to roll out startups that integrate and deliver value around their data services offering.

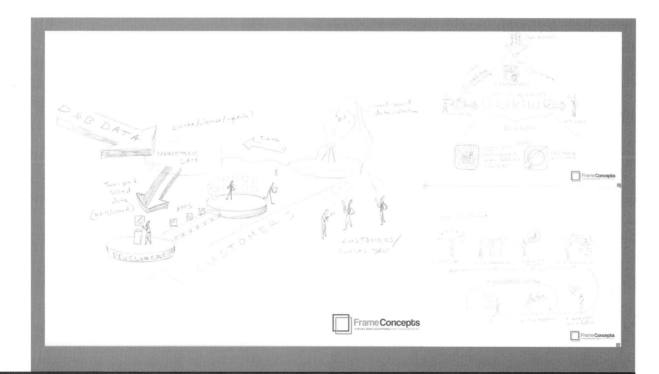

# COLLABORATIVE TOOL GOES THROUGH VISUAL IDEATION PHASE

We already had developed some innovation visualization tools for the spare parts management program, and now the topic turned to the outage process for a nuclear reactor. How could everyone in the organization come to terms with staffing the outage with the relevant accredited technicians, up-to-date repair tools, and the requisite spare parts so that the outage process would go smoothly? First, the idea has to be crystallized, as shown in the following ideation sketch.

BEFORE THE OUTAGE

PROVIDE VISIBILITY BETWEEN CUSTOMER AND GE·HITACHI

- Schedule of Outages
- Plant Components + Tools
- Required Training
- MPLs

AFTER AN OUTAGE

GEH MANAGEMENT REVIEWS DATA AND GATHERS INTELLIGENCE FOR FUTURE OUTAGES. CUSTOMER IS INVITED TO REVIEW AS WELL.

TAI - MAC VACUUM

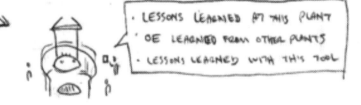

CENTRAL GEH PLANNING TOOL

GEH ENGINEERS ARE ABLE TO
PREPARE FOR UPCOMING SERVICES,
AND SEND QUALIFIED PERSONNEL
TO CUSTOMER PLANT

- Resource management
- Scheduling
- Training & Certification

## DURING AN OUTAGE

- LESSONS LEARNED AT THIS PLANT
- OE LEARNED FROM OTHER PLANTS
- LESSONS LEARNED WITH THIS TOOL

ENABLE GEH ENGINEERS TO INTEGRATE
KNOWLEDGE STORED IN DATABASES WHILE
AT THE JOB SITE

GEH DBS

# IT/NETWORKING INDUSTRY VISUAL SOLUTIONS

- Predictive Analytics Firm Debriefs Analysts Visually

- Large Networking Vendor Visualizes Best Practices for Setting Up Network

- IT Network Data Visualization: Top of Mind for CIOs

# PREDICTIVE ANALYTICS FIRM DEBRIEFS ANALYSTS VISUALLY

In an unusual move, the client leveraged an infographic to showcase specifically to analysts, with the numbers and research feeding the solution and the unique benefits of their approach. This visual showcase worked as a way to solicit interest in the analyst community itself and also as a debriefing tool to walk them through the approach. The infographic communication vehicle was so powerful that the analyst receiving the infographic debriefing reached out to Frame Concepts to discuss how their research practice could also be presented visually.

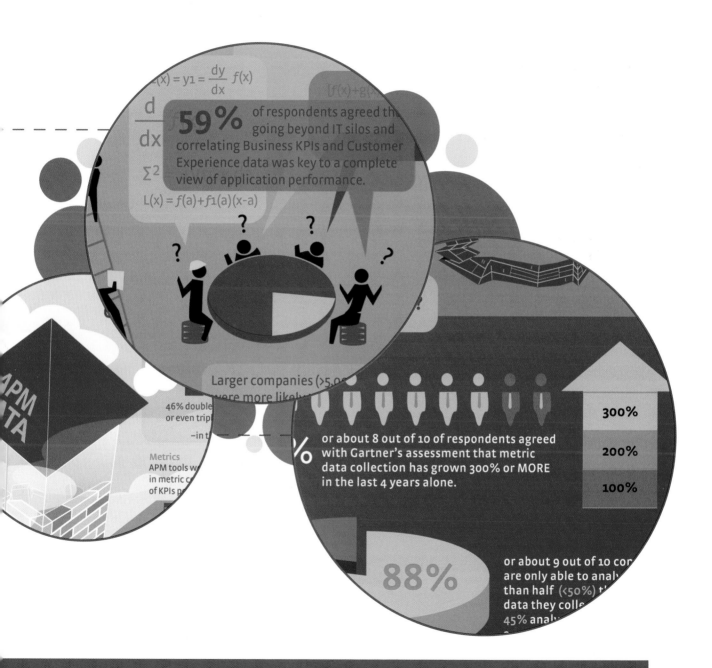

# LARGE NETWORKING VENDOR VISUALIZES BEST PRACTICES FOR SETTING UP NETWORK

Led by powerful research, this infographic was formed with a visual cutaway of a building to drive the context for a host of practical steps one should consider when setting up a new network in new construction. While the facts and figures were quite broad, with intelligent information design, the important drives were visually placed in conceptual buckets, subtly suggesting how the client's offerings were relevant to the concerns surfaced by the research.

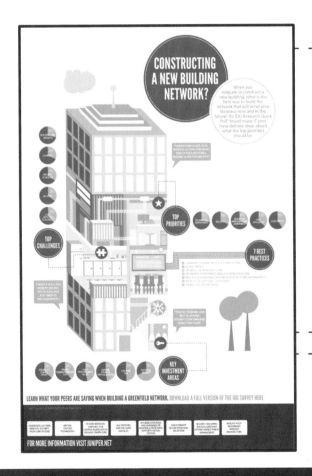

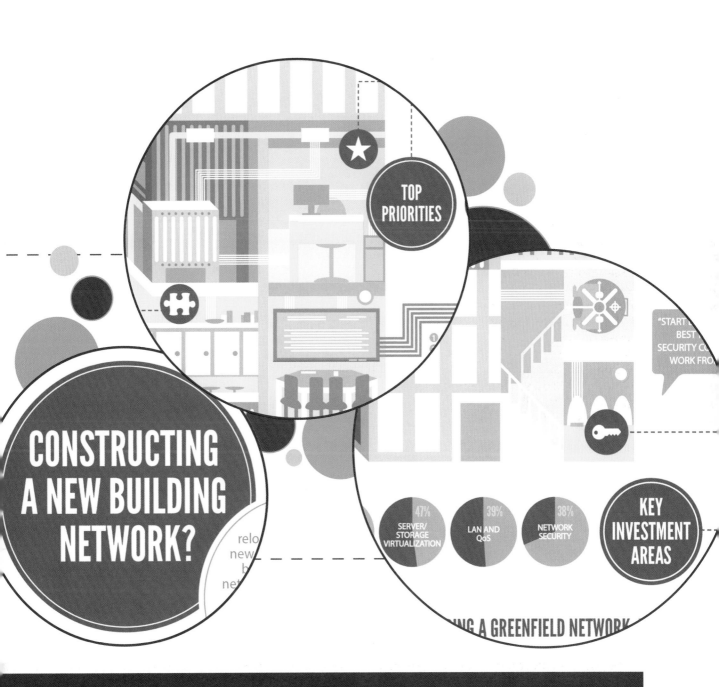

TOP PRIORITIES

"START [...] BEST SECURITY C[...] WORK FRO[...]"

# CONSTRUCTING A NEW BUILDING NETWORK?

relo[...]
new[...]
b[...]
net[...]

| 47% SERVER/ STORAGE VIRTUALIZATION | 39% LAN AND QoS | 38% NETWORK SECURITY | KEY INVESTMENT AREAS |

[...]NG A GREENFIELD NETWORK

# IT NETWORK DATA VISUALIZATION: TOP OF MIND FOR CIOS

IT networks can keep a CIO up at night. A large enterprise IT network data company sponsored research to poll CIOs about their concerns and where the solution may lie in this visualization of the poll results. While aspects of the network can be quite technical—security, virtualization, the cloud, big data— the concerns that can have a real impact on business performance are shared by the entire business.

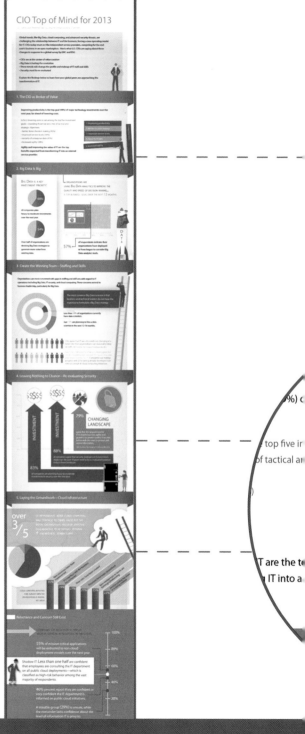

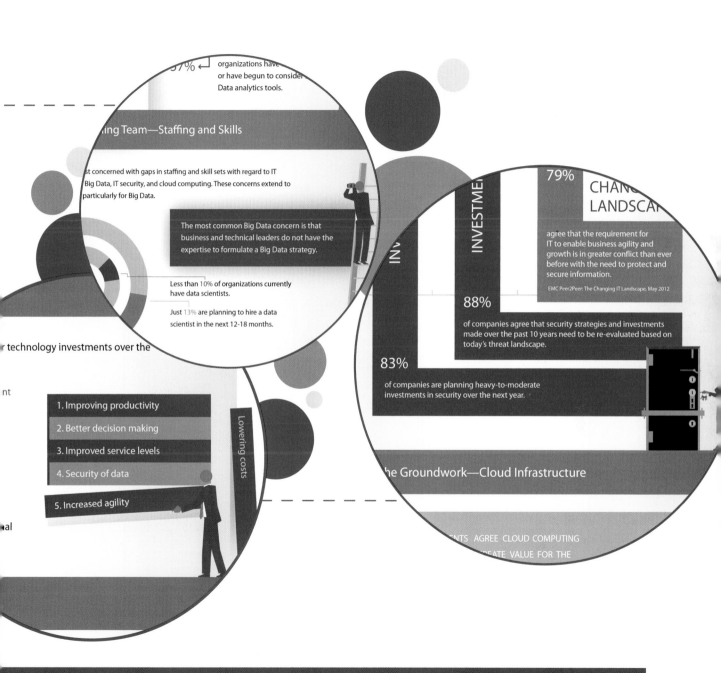

57% organizations have
or have begun to consider
Data analytics tools.

### ...ing Team—Staffing and Skills

...st concerned with gaps in staffing and skill sets with regard to IT
...Big Data, IT security, and cloud computing. These concerns extend to
...particularly for Big Data.

The most common Big Data concern is that
business and technical leaders do not have the
expertise to formulate a Big Data strategy.

Less than 10% of organizations currently
have data scientists.

Just 13% are planning to hire a data
scientist in the next 12-18 months.

...r technology investments over the

...nt

1. Improving productivity
2. Better decision making
3. Improved service levels
4. Security of data
5. Increased agility

Lowering costs

...al

79% CHAN...
LANDSCA...

INVESTME...

agree that the requirement for
IT to enable business agility and
growth is in greater conflict than ever
before with the need to protect and
secure information.

EMC Peer2Peer: The Changing IT Landscape, May 2012

88%

of companies agree that security strategies and investments
made over the past 10 years need to be re-evaluated based on
today's threat landscape.

83%

of companies are planning heavy-to-moderate
investments in security over the next year.

### ...he Groundwork—Cloud Infrastructure

...NTS AGREE CLOUD COMPUTING
...EATE VALUE FOR THE

# MANAGEMENT CONSULTING INDUSTRY VISUAL SOLUTIONS

- Reputation Consultancy Visualizes Results Against Bottom Line

- Management Consulting Firm New Corporate Performance Model Gets Visualization

- Marketing Consulting Firms Gets Clients Onboard with Automation Process

# REPUTATION CONSULTANCY VISUALIZES RESULTS AGAINST BOTTOM LINE

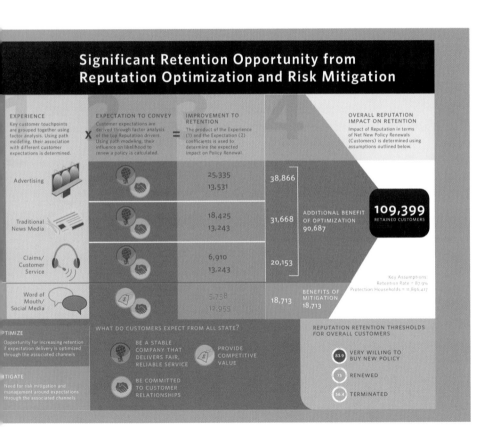

With social channels exponentially growing in traffic, this reputation consulting firm can tie the good and the bad together and show how making the right corrective actions can help the bottom line. The following slide shows recommendations through clever use of iconography.

# MANAGEMENT CONSULTING FIRM NEW CORPORATE PERFORMANCE MODEL GETS VISUALIZATION

A global consulting firm had come up with a new cross-comparative business performance model that pivoted around the concept of a miracle worker. The model leveraged actual historical performance data on multiple companies that displayed how their unique model captured relevant causal factors that other models did not. The following slide displays an early-stage speculative data visualization.

SPECULATIVE
DESIGN MOCK-UP

**Return on Assets for Miracle Worker Co.**
(a company that consistently ranks in the 9th decile of performance among all publicly traded U.S.-based companies)

⑨ Rank in the MW focal 9th decile　#️⃣ Rank lower than 9th decile　▬ ▬ ROA trend line　　ROA variation

Miracle Worker streak begins

RETURN ON ASSETS

# MARKETING CONSULTING FIRM GETS CLIENTS ONBOARD WITH AUTOMATION PROCESS

The marketing automation industry is as complex as any software-based platform service. With software vendor selection and working out workflows and triggers and matching the right content with the right stage in the sales funnel, the whole process can be dizzying to the uninitiated. The consulting firm demystified the setup and strategy process with a clear, engaging, and fun visual walkthrough of the key process steps in this colorful pictogram.

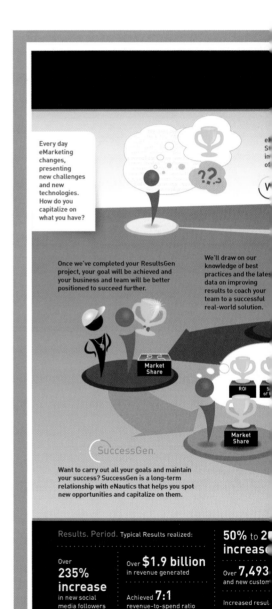

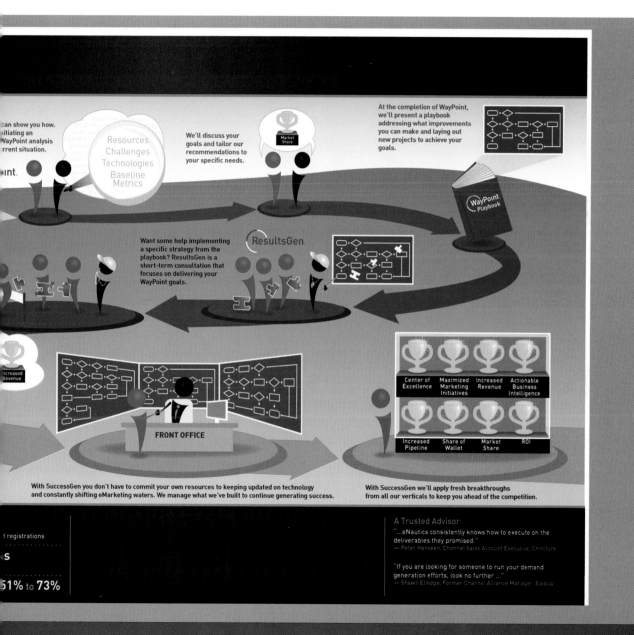

can show you how.
itiating an
WayPoint analysis
rrent situation.

Resources
Challenges
Technologies
Baseline
Metrics

We'll discuss your goals and tailor our recommendations to your specific needs.

At the completion of WayPoint, we'll present a playbook addressing what improvements you can make and laying out new projects to achieve your goals.

WayPoint Playbook

Want some help implementing a specific strategy from the playbook? ResultsGen is a short-term consultation that focuses on delivering your WayPoint goals.

ResultsGen

FRONT OFFICE

| | | | |
|---|---|---|---|
| Center of Excellence | Maximized Marketing Initiatives | Increased Revenue | Actionable Business Intelligence |
| Increased Pipeline | Share of Wallet | Market Share | ROI |

With SuccessGen you don't have to commit your own resources to keeping updated on technology and constantly shifting eMarketing waters. We manage what we've built to continue generating success.

With SuccessGen we'll apply fresh breakthroughs from all our verticals to keep you ahead of the competition.

t registrations

s

51% to 73%

A Trusted Advisor
"...eNautics consistently knows how to execute on the deliverables they promised."
— Peter Hanseen, Channel Sales Account Executive, Omniture

"If you are looking for someone to run your demand generation efforts, look no further ..."
— Shawn Elledge, Former Channel Alliance Manager, Eloqua

# MEDIA INDUSTRY VISUAL SOLUTIONS

- Digital Media Company Disturbs Ad Week with Infographic Series

- Independent Film Platform Startup Shakes Things Up with Pictogram

- Analytics Firm New User Interface Integrates TV and Online Metrics

# DIGITAL MEDIA COMPANY DISTURBS AD WEEK WITH INFOGRAPHIC SERIES

The digital and younger division of a large TV and radio conglomerate that actually competes against the parent company for ad spend during the annual Ad Week buying frenzy wanted their metrics to stand out. To stand out during the three-day event, three compelling infographics were created showcasing their attractive demographics. They released one each day from Monday to Wednesday. In a field of metric-filled spreadsheets, they stood out.

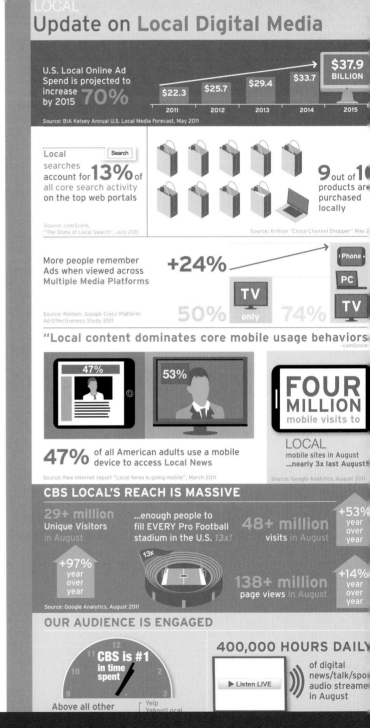

# Compared to the rest of the web,
# THE LOCAL AUDIENCE IS...

## AFFLUENT

Household income of **$75K+**

Household income of **$100K+**

**12X** More likely to fly **3-4 times/year**

**47%**

**30%**

**2X** more likely to **BUY A HOME** in the next 6 month

## POLITICALLY ACTIVE

to be **undecided voters**

make political **DONATIONS**

Visit **Political Sites**

**Voted**

**ALWAYS VOTE** in Presidential Elections

Voted

Nearly **3X** more likely

**2X** more likely

**2X** more likely

**17%** more likely

## SPORTS CRAZY

ave spent **$500–$999** online for ports/Entertainment Tickets within the last 6 months

**ATTEND A PRO-SPORTS EVENT** in the next 6 months

STATE

Purchas **College/Amate Sports Tickets Onlin** in the next 6 month

**3X** more likely

Nearly **3X** more likely

**2X** more likely

## TECH SAVVY

**Own a digital E-Reader/iPad**

Be the **FIRST TO BUY** the **LATEST GADGET**

Read **News, Weather info** on a **mobile device** within the next month

**2X** more likely

**68%** more likely

**4X** more likely

ource: comScore Plan Metrix, August 2011. Site Audience Profile: CBS Local, Adults 18+ US Residents

**OCAL**

## LOCAL Commerce

**U.S. Daily Deals Market**

**$873 MILLION** in 2010

**$4.2 BILLION** in 2015

Source: BIA/Kelsey: U.S. deals forecast, September 2011

**OVER 26 MILLION** people have purchased a Daily Deal

= 1 million

**> 50%** of all Daily Deal users have bought from **3 OR MORE Deal Providers**
Source: CityPocket

**81%** of advertiser have not **yet** participated in a deals program

Source: Borrell Associates/Pressilaff Interactiv Revenue survey, insideRadio.com September 20

Source: CityPockets

## LOCAL Offers INSIGHTS

**70%** of CBS Local Offers Subscribers are **NEW CUSTOMERS** for the Merchant

**15%** of CBS Local Offer Merchant **HAVE RUN A DEA MORE THA ONC**

Local listings are the new Word-Of-Mouth marketing... 7 out of 10 online consumers **trust opinions** of unknown user reviews

Source: Nielsen, July 2009

**Nearly ALL CONSUMERS** go online when researching products/services in their local area

**97%** use online media

Source: BIA/Kelsey and Constat User View Wave VII, March 2010

### LOCAL Pages
**Top Performing Categories to Targe**

Automotive Sales and Services

Arts and Entertainment

Construction and Remodeling

Health and Medical

Attorneys and Legal Services

Personal Services

## LOCAL Pages INSIGHTS

Local Pages Seminar

**CALENDAR**

**20%** of attendees sign up on the spot

**+15%** more within 1 week

**7%** of Pages clients are in the **Automotive Sales**

**90%** of Pages campaigns are g to over-delive

# INDEPENDENT FILM PLATFORM STARTUP SHAKES THINGS UP WITH PICTOGRAM

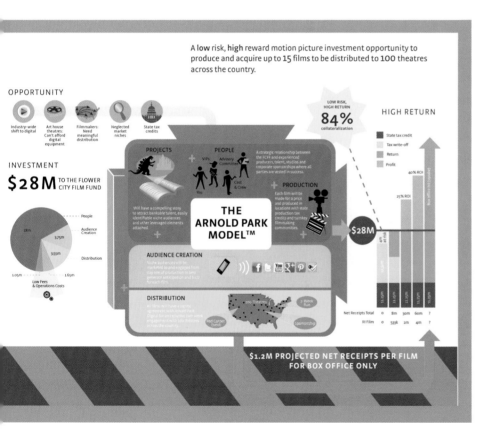

The independent film industry has always been challenged to get movies funded, secure movie theatre distribution, and earn a profit. This startup made a new model connecting new investors with independent filmmakers through a new platform that offered the latest film projector technology to smaller movie houses and clarified the return on investment numbers in the murky world of the film industry. The one-page pictogram was key to showcasing the model to early adopters.

# ANALYTICS FIRM NEW USER INTERFACE INTEGRATES TV AND ONLINE METRICS

Breaking new ground by offering campaign performance both on TV and online metrics from one source, a new data visualization design and user interface was created to highlight to its beta customers the inherent value of the new integrated platform.

# PHARMACEUTICAL INDUSTRY VISUAL SOLUTIONS

- Large Pharmaceutical Merger Leverages Pictogram to Get Staff Onboard

- Improving Prescription Delivery with Tablets

- New Allergy Over-the-Counter Drug Gets Interactive Engagement

# LARGE PHARMACEUTICAL MERGER LEVERAGES PICTOGRAM TO GET STAFF ONBOARD

Two large pharmaceuticals were going through a merger, and there were significant benefits to be had on a global scale for the employees in both organizations. The following presentation offered a pictogram to tie the framework together and show the exciting opportunities this merger offered.

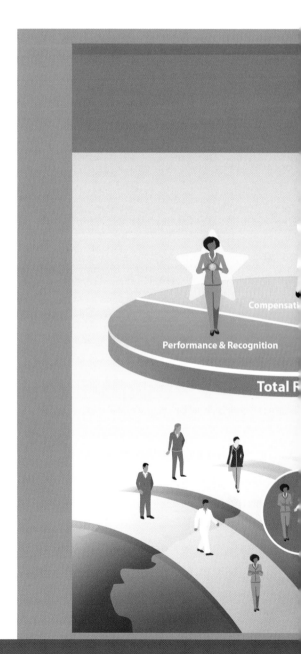

### Performance & Recognition

- Performance Management Program (PMP)
- Goal Setting
- Feedback and Coaching

### Development & Career

- Learning and Training
- Individual Development Plans
- Career Paths

### Compensation & Benefits

Global Job and Pay Framework
Base Salary and Incentives
Comprehensive Benefits Package

# IMPROVING PRESCRIPTION DELIVERY WITH TABLETS

The myriad ways tablets can improve drug and healthcare delivery through digital means is visually captured, along with the metric-based benefits in this engaging infographic.

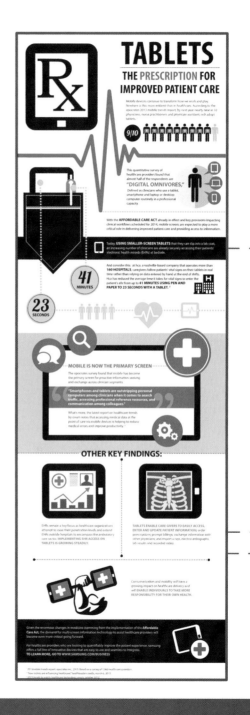

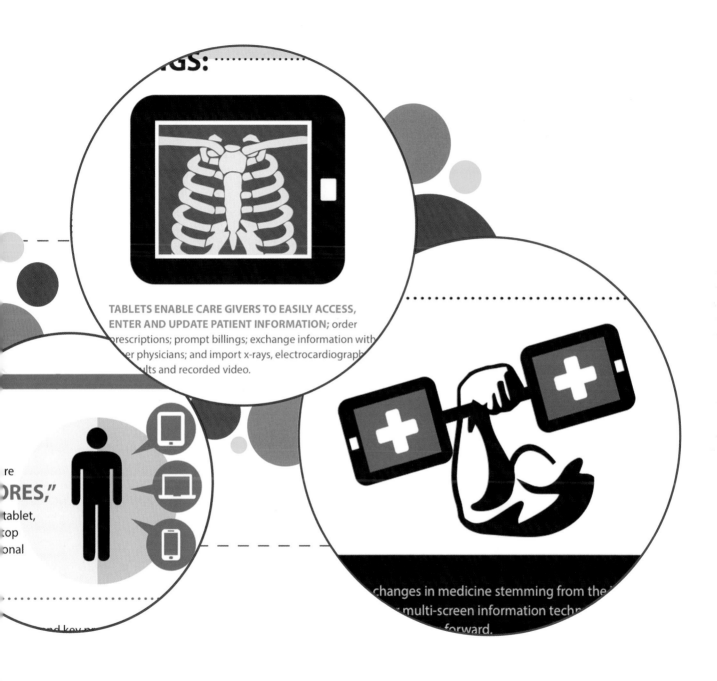

...GS: ............

**TABLETS ENABLE CARE GIVERS TO EASILY ACCESS, ENTER AND UPDATE PATIENT INFORMATION;** order prescriptions; prompt billings; exchange information with er physicians; and import x-rays, electrocardiograph lts and recorded video.

re

**DRES,"**

tablet,

top

onal

changes in medicine stemming from the multi-screen information techn forward.

# NEW ALLERGY OVER-THE-COUNTER DRUG GETS INTERACTIVE ENGAGEMENT

An allergy startup had brought a new over-the-counter allergy drug and wanted to show its patients how each of the natural ingredients delivered value. This simple interactive infographic was placed on its home page to increase click-through engagement and conversion.

arn more!

NETTLE          EYEBRIGHT          MENTHOL

VITAMIN C

# PROFESSIONAL SERVICES INDUSTRY VISUAL SOLUTIONS

- Marketing Automation Firm Visualizes Its Marketing Automation Process

- Architecture Association Poster-Foldout Shows Community Value

- Accounting Association Visually Celebrated 125th Anniversary with iPad Dynamic Visualization

# MARKETING AUTOMATION FIRM VISUALIZES ITS MARKETING AUTOMATION PROCESS

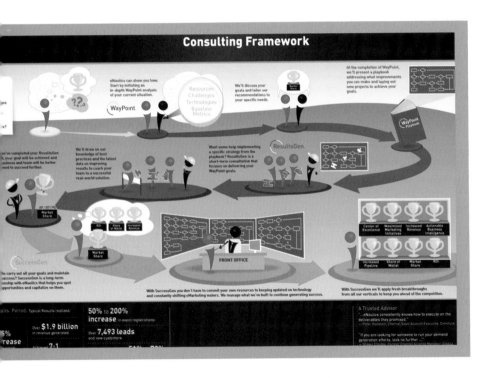

Marketing automation is all the rage, but with a host of complex software platforms, sophisticated workflows, and lead nurturing systems—the whole point of the program can be lost on the potential buyer. This client leveraged a lush pictogram to reinforce how simple their approach is so their own clients appreciate the value and ease of integration.

# ARCHITECTURE ASSOCIATION POSTER-FOLDOUT SHOWS COMMUNITY VALUE

The Architecture Association wanted to showcase the levels of value that the profession of architecture delivers to the community at a large congress event. The challenge was to provide a large poster-format explanatory infographic that enabled the congress members to walk away from the event with the foldout tucked under their arms. This was designed cleverly by weaving the explanatory infographic across the folds so it functioned in both applications.

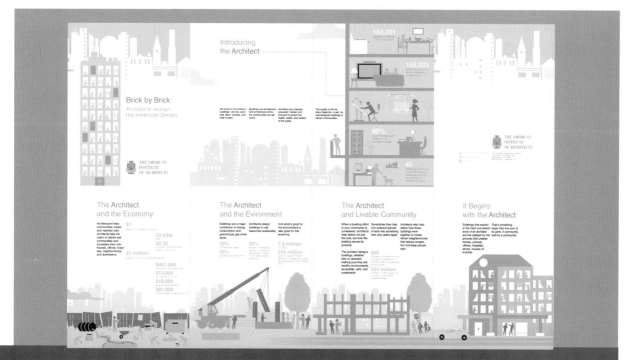

# ACCOUNTING ASSOCIATION VISUALLY CELEBRATED 125TH ANNIVERSARY WITH IPAD DYNAMIC VISUALIZATION

The rich and illustrious history of the CPA organization needed a visual home. Both a desktop and tablet version were created that allowed visitors to navigate a dynamic timeline to engage and interact with a multimedia tour of its compelling historic milestones.

1887 - 2012

HERITA

1885

timeline celebrating 125 years of the AICPA and the accounting profession

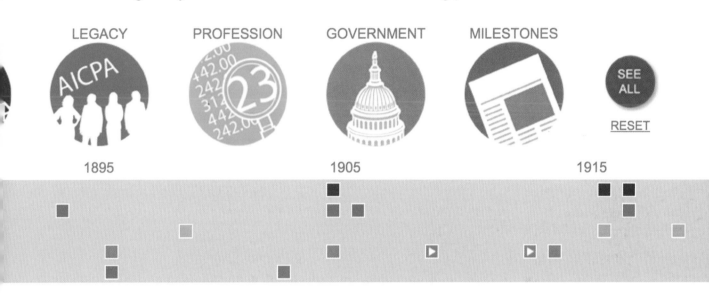

LEGACY     PROFESSION     GOVERNMENT     MILESTONES

SEE ALL

RESET

1895     1905     1915

START EXPLORING

Scroll through the bar above and click the entries, or isolate a category with the buttons at top.

You'll find photos, videos and the stories that detail the rich heritage of AICPA and the accounting profession.

CELEBRATING

# RESEARCH INDUSTRY VISUAL SOLUTIONS

- Research Infographic Showcases Best Practices for New Construction Network Deployment

- Data Visualization Highlights Management Consulting Firm Research on New Business Performance Model

- Financial Data Firm Small Business Health Index Research Report Gets Iconic Treatment

# RESEARCH INFOGRAPHIC SHOWCASES
# BEST PRACTICES FOR NEW CONSTRUCTION
# NETWORK DEPLOYMENT

A large networking vendor sponsored custom research on the topic of best practices around new construction and network setup and deployment. In order to drive marketplace engagement with the findings, the following infographic highlighted the key recommendations and best practice tips in the visual context of new building construction. This is an effective research communications strategy, as it pulls the audience into some of the more provocative points visually and causes them to click through to download the research and also review the technical solutions that the research sponsor offers against these conclusions.

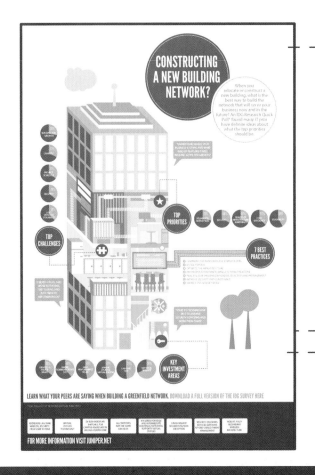

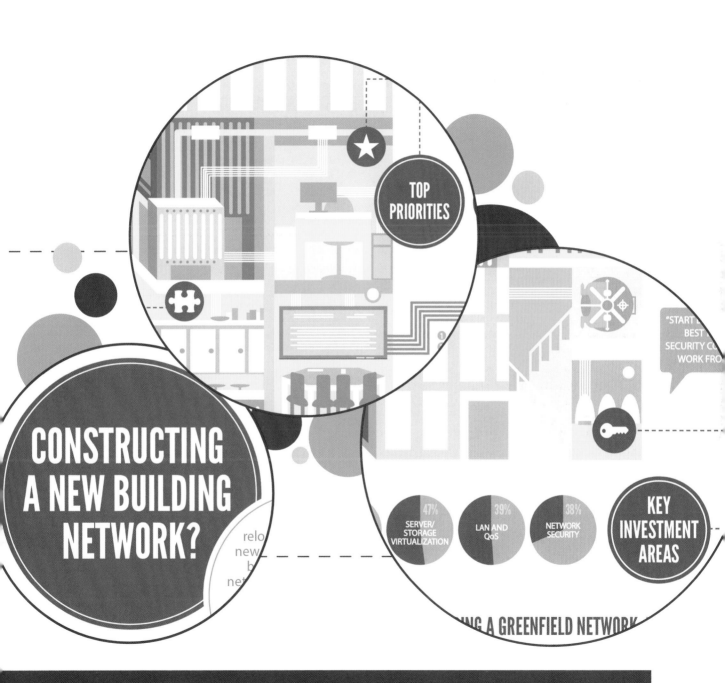

CONSTRUCTING A NEW BUILDING NETWORK?

TOP PRIORITIES

KEY INVESTMENT AREAS

47% SERVER/STORAGE VIRTUALIZATION

39% LAN AND QoS

38% NETWORK SECURITY

"START BEST SECURITY C WORK FRO

ING A GREENFIELD NETWORK

# DATA VISUALIZATION HIGHLIGHTS MANAGEMENT CONSULTING FIRM RESEARCH ON NEW BUSINESS PERFORMANCE MODEL

A management consulting firm's research suggested that some important comparative variables were not being integrated into business performance analysis. A new concept centered on the notion of a "miracle worker" was generated, and research proved that it was a more effective predictor of business performance. The trick now was to get clients onboard with the model, so the following speculative dashboard visualization was developed to make the visual case.

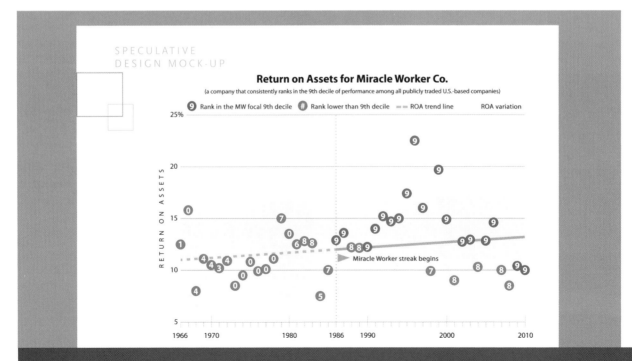

# FINANCIAL DATA FIRM SMALL BUSINESS HEALTH INDEX RESEARCH REPORT GETS ICONIC TREATMENT

This client does a lot of research around influencing factors that have an impact on small businesses. This research, in the form of a monthly report, was labeled the Small Business Health Index. To help their audiences to quickly appreciate the monthly findings visually, a report template was designed that took advantage of clever use of iconography.

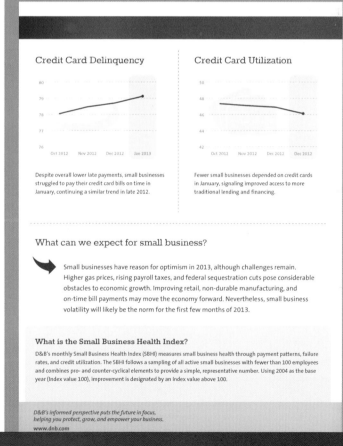

### Credit Card Delinquency

Despite overall lower late payments, small businesses struggled to pay their credit card bills on time in January, continuing a similar trend in late 2012.

### Credit Card Utilization

Fewer small businesses depended on credit cards in January, signaling improved access to more traditional lending and financing.

### What can we expect for small business?

Small businesses have reason for optimism in 2013, although challenges remain. Higher gas prices, rising payroll taxes, and federal sequestration cuts pose considerable obstacles to economic growth. Improving retail, non-durable manufacturing, and on-time bill payments may move the economy forward. Nevertheless, small business volatility will likely be the norm for the first few months of 2013.

### What is the Small Business Health Index?

D&B's monthly Small Business Health Index (SBHI) measures small business health through payment patterns, failure rates, and credit utilization. The SBHI follows a sampling of all active small businesses with fewer than 100 employees and combines pro- and counter-cyclical elements to provide a simple, representative number. Using 2004 as the base year (Index value 100), improvement is designated by an Index value above 100.

*D&B's informed perspective puts the future in focus, helping you protect, grow, and empower your business.*
www.dnb.com

# RETAIL AND ECOMMERCE INDUSTRY VISUAL SOLUTIONS

- Digital Media Firm Visually Shakes Things Up at Ad Week Trade Show

- Tablet Maker Showcases How Tablets Are Reinventing the Retail Customer Experience

- Translating Super Bowl Ads Metrics to Social Channel Performance

# DIGITAL MEDIA FIRM VISUALLY SHAKES THINGS UP AT AD WEEK TRADE SHOW

A digital agency has impressive ecommerce metrics. The problem is that during their annual Ad Week trade show, when the big brands are looking to direct their online spending, they think about TV and radio. To bring their impressive ecommerce metrics, typically buried in spreadsheets, to the fore-front, a three-day infographic series was created. They got noticed.

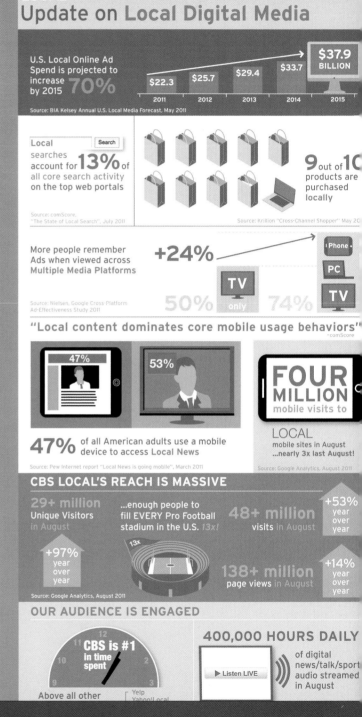

# Compared to the rest of the web,
# THE LOCAL AUDIENCE IS...

## AFFLUENT

Household income of **$75K+**

Household income of **$100K+**

**12X** More likely to fly 3–4 times/year

**47%**  **30%**

**2X** more likely to **BUY A HOME** in the next 6 month

## POLITICALLY ACTIVE

to be **undecided voters**

make political **DONATIONS**

Visit **Political Sites**

**Voted**

**ALWAYS VOTE** in Presidential Elections

**Voted**

Nearly **3X** more likely

**2X** more likely

**2X** more likely

**17%** more likely

## SPORTS CRAZY

**STATE**

Have spent **$500–$999 online for Sports/Entertainment Tickets** within the last 6 months

**ATTEND A PRO-SPORTS EVENT** in the next 6 months

**Purchas College/Amate Sports Tickets Onlin** in the next 6 mont

**3X** more likely

Nearly **3X** more likely

**2X** more likely

## TECH SAVVY

**NEWS**

Own a digital **E-Reader/iPad**

Be the **FIRST TO BUY** the **LATEST GADGET**

Read **News, Weather info** on a **mobile device** within the next month

**2X** more likely

**68%** more likely

**4X** more likely

Source: comScore Plan Metrix, August 2011. Site Audience Profile: CBS Local, Adults 18+ US Residents

## LOCAL

---

# LOCAL Commerce

## U.S. Daily Deals Market

**$873 MILLION** in 2010

**$4.2 BILLION** in 2015

Source: BIA/Kelsey: U.S. deals forecast, September 2011

Source: CityPock

**OVER 26 MILLION** people have purchased a Daily Deal

= 1 million

**> 50%** of all Daily Dea users have bought from **3 OR MORE Deal Providers**
Source: CityPock

**81%** of advertiser have not **yet** participate in a deals program
Source: Borrell Associates/Presslaff Interact Revenue survey, InsideRadio.com September 2

## LOCAL Offers INSIGHTS

**70%** of CBS Local Offers Subscribers are **NEW CUSTOMERS** for the Merchant

**15%** of CBS Local Offe Merchan **HAVE RUN A DEA MORE THA ONC**

**Local listings are the new Word-Of-Mouth marketing... 7 out of 10** online consumers **trust opinions of unknown user reviews**
Source: Nielsen, July 2009

**Nearly ALL CONSUMERS** go online when researching products/services in their local area

**97%** use online media

Source: BIA/Kelsey and Constat User View Wave VII, March 2010

### LOCAL Pages
**Top Performing Categories to Targ**

- Automotive Sales and Services
- Arts and Entertainment
- Construction and Remodeling
- Health and Medical
- Attorneys and Legal Services
- Personal Services

## LOCAL Pages INSIGHTS

Local Pages Seminar

**CALENDAR**
M TW TH FR SA SU

**20%** of attendees sign up on the spot

**+15%** more within 1 week

**7%** of Pages clients are in the **Automotive Sales**

**90%** of Pages campaigns ar ng to over-deliv

---

Created By: FrameCon

# TABLET MAKER SHOWCASES HOW TABLETS ARE REINVENTING THE RETAIL CUSTOMER EXPERIENCE

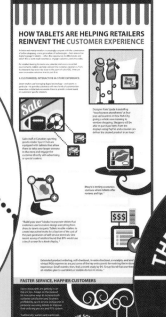

A provocative visual journey literally showing how tablets are having a dramatic impact on the customer experience was created. While infographics excel as making the conceptual benefits visually tangible, in this case the physicality of the tablet helped drive the visual story.

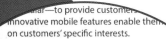

...iliar—to provide customer...
innovative mobile features enable them...
on customers' specific interests.

Sales staff at Canadian sporting goods retailer Sport Chek are equipped with **tablets that allow them to take over larger screens in the store** and engage the customer directly with advertising or special content.

**THE NEW SOLUTION**

Perform tableside
with a tablet and
essential: tablet
easily carry the
screen size an
POS menu t
clearly; a
effici

# TRANSLATING SUPER BOWL ADS METRICS TO SOCIAL CHANNEL PERFORMANCE

While all of us marvel at the amount retailers will spend on Super Bowl one-minute ads, we suspect that behind the seemingly exorbitant spend, it translates in numbers. A video analytics firm took this intuition one step further and showed, through a simple data visualization, how the social channels surrounding the television ads are having a big impact on brand awareness and recall, which will translate at the cash register. Also note that not all visuals have to be illustrative or iconic; sometimes it's good to let the numbers tell the story.

**Super Bowl Ad Rankings**
Earned Media

### Calculating Earned ROI of Super Bowl Ads

| | Advertisement | Earned Media* | Cumulative Viewership** |
|---|---|---|---|
| 1. | Honda CR-V 2012 - "Matthew's Day Off" | $2,243,275 | 14,762,276 |
| 2. | Acura NSX - "Transactions" | $2,175,464 | 18,534,151 |
| 3. | Chrysler - "Halftime in America" | $973,627 | 7,677,968 |
| 4. | VW "The Dog Strikes Back" | $754,369 | 9,471,291 |
| 5. | Fiat - "500 Abrath" | $490,451 | 7,428,379 |
| 6. | Audi - "Vampire Party" | $461,180 | 7,214,068 |
| 7. | Chevy Silverado "End of the World" | $450,587 | 6,934,674 |
| 8. | M&M'S - "Just My Shell" | $421,461 | 12,972,847 |
| 9. | Toyota Camry "It's Reinvented!" | $364,159 | 5,696,402 |
| 10. | Pepsi - "King's Court" | $285,833 | 4,471,186 |
| | **Top 10 Cumulative:** | $8,620,406 | 95,163,242 |
| | **All Super Bowl Ads Cumulative** | $11,114,526 | 148,636,444 |

**The Super Bowl "Bounce"**

| **TOTAL VALUE CREATED** | |
|---|---|
| Pre-Game | Post-Game |
| $2,153,746 | $9,514,420 |

| **TOTAL AD VIEWERSHIP** | |
|---|---|
| Pre-Game | Post-Game |
| 40,465,557 | 108,170,887 |

Social Recall Auto Ads***

| | Brand | Theme |
|---|---|---|
| 1. | Audi | 1. "Vampire" AUDI |
| 2. | Volkswagen | 2. "Dog" VOLKSWAGEN |
| 3. | Toyota | 3. "Jerry Seinfeld" ACURA |
| 4. | Acura | 4. "Ferris Bueller" HONDA |
| 5. | Honda | 5. "America" CHRYSLER |
| 6. | Chrysler | 6. "Reinvented" TOYOTA |

Source:

# SOFTWARE INDUSTRY VISUAL SOLUTIONS

- Global ERP Software Vendor Engages with Shipping Analogy

- Large Enterprise Software Vendor Showcases Productivity in Cloud

- Security Software Vendor Shows Right Approach to Patch Management

# GLOBAL ERP SOFTWARE VENDOR ENGAGES WITH SHIPPING ANALOGY

While the sophistication of its reporting tools and the data feeds integrated to make accurate robust forecasts can be quite technical, this software firm brings in the business user with a fun and provocative meandering ship analogy with a playful financial forecasting shipping analogy infographic.

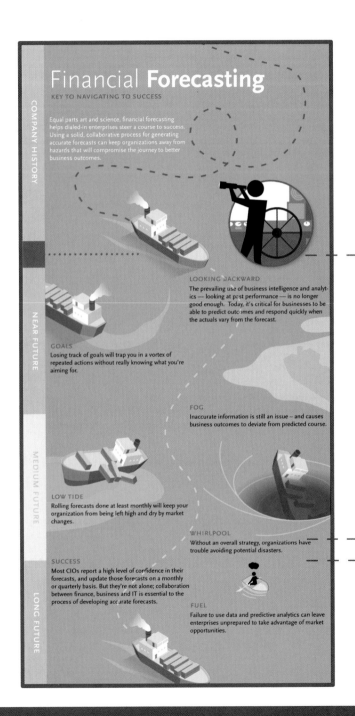

# Financial **Forecasting**

KEY TO NAVIGATING TO SUCCESS

Equal parts art and science, financial forecasting helps dialed-in enterprises steer a course to success. Using a solid, collaborative process for generating accurate forecasts can keep organizations away from hazards that will compromise the journey to better business outcomes.

COMPANY HISTORY

NEAR FUTURE

MEDIUM FUTURE

LONG FUTURE

LOOKING BACKWARD
The prevailing use of business intelligence and analytics — looking at past performance — is no longer good enough. Today, it's critical for businesses to be able to predict outcomes and respond quickly when the actuals vary from the forecast.

GOALS
Losing track of goals will trap you in a vortex of repeated actions without really knowing what you're aiming for.

FOG
Inaccurate information is still an issue – and causes business outcomes to deviate from predicted course.

LOW TIDE
Rolling forecasts done at least monthly will keep your organization from being left high and dry by market changes.

WHIRLPOOL
Without an overall strategy, organizations have trouble avoiding potential disasters.

SUCCESS
Most CIOs report a high level of confidence in their forecasts, and update those forecasts on a monthly or quarterly basis. But they're not alone; collaboration between finance, business and IT is essential to the process of developing accurate forecasts.

FUEL
Failure to use data and predictive analytics can leave enterprises unprepared to take advantage of market opportunities.

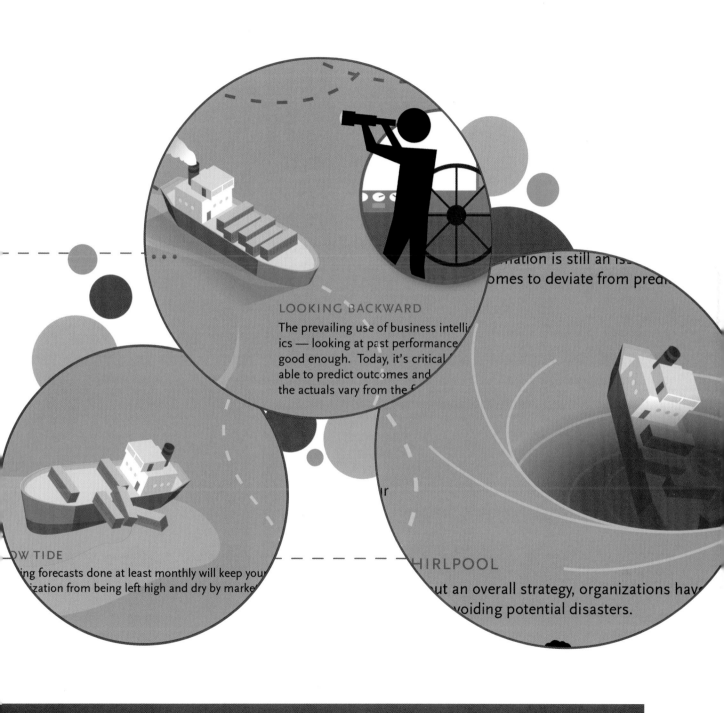

LOOKING BACKWARD

The prevailing use of business intelli
ics — looking at past performance
good enough. Today, it's critical
able to predict outcomes and
the actuals vary from the f

...ation is still an iss
...omes to deviate from prea

...OW TIDE

...ing forecasts done at least monthly will keep your
...ization from being left high and dry by marke

...HIRLPOOL

...ut an overall strategy, organizations hav
...voiding potential disasters.

# LARGE ENTERPRISE SOFTWARE VENDOR SHOWCASES PRODUCTIVITY IN CLOUD

This research-based infographic helped the software vendor showcase how cloud-based delivery of productivity applications is lowering the workload for the IT department and allowing them to focus on more strategic efforts. This particular example uses a clever balance of data visualization, iconography, and illustration to make the visual narrative drive to this conclusion.

## REACHING FOR THE BRASS RING OF PRODUCTIVITY IN CLOUD APPS

Organizations are turning To cloud-based deployments

Almost all IT leaders say at least a portion of their workforce would benefit from the ability to use enterprise-grade productivity applications anywhere, anytime and on any device. (98%)

### 1 STRATEGIC IMPORTANCE

Consensus: It's strategically important to provide employees with anywhere/anytime mobile access to enterprise-grade productivity applications.

**81%**

Critically Important
Very Important
Somewhat Important
Not Very Important
Not Important At All

### 2 WHAT'S IMPORTANT

**55%** knowing where the data is: access and transparency

**58%** the vendor's financial stability

**82%** Control over data ownership

Access to enterprise-grade applications anywhere, anytime, on any device would ease many commonly felt pain points, according to IT leaders. And the cloud is the overwhelming choice to deploy these high-grade applications. The ultimate goal: to make it less challenging to get enterprise data into the hands and devices of employees.

### 3 WE CAN DO THIS

Only 8% say it's "extememly challenging" to deploy such a solution.

Extremely challenging 8%
Not at all challenging 4%
Not very challenging 10%
Very challenging 19%
Somewhat challenging 59%

### 4 RELIEF

Mobile access to apps and data frees up IT for strategic work by easing these pain points:

Too many manual tasks
Lack of skilled workers
Overworked employees
Complexity
Employee turnover

IDG Research Services, April 2013

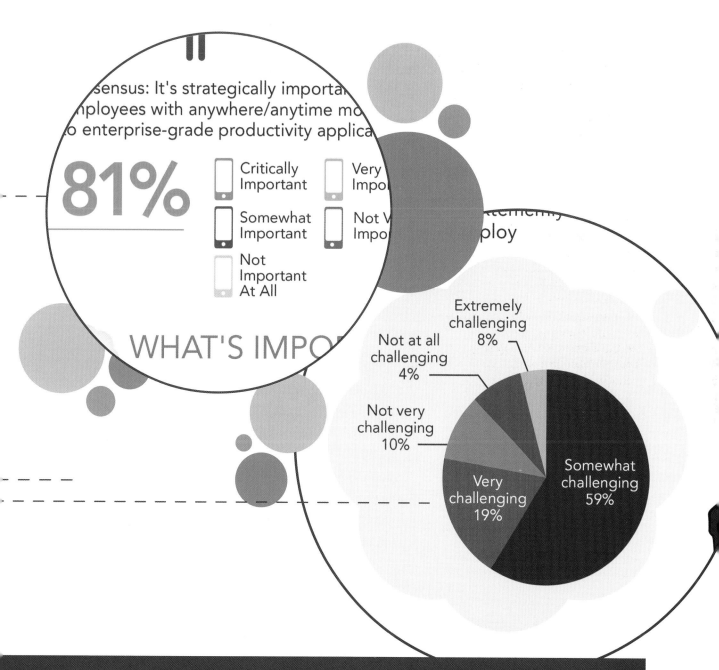

...sensus: It's strategically importan...
...ployees with anywhere/anytime mo...
...o enterprise-grade productivity applica...

# 81%

- Critically Important
- Very Impo...
- Somewhat Important
- Not V... Impo...
- Not Important At All

...tremely ...ploy

WHAT'S IMPO...

Extremely challenging 8%

Not at all challenging 4%

Not very challenging 10%

Very challenging 19%

Somewhat challenging 59%

# SECURITY SOFTWARE VENDOR SHOWS RIGHT APPROACH TO PATCH MANAGEMENT

This software vendor cleverly lays out the case for effective patch management, citing relevant statistics around the rise of cyber attacks and the challenge of manually managing the process, and ultimately argues for an automated approach to solve the problem.

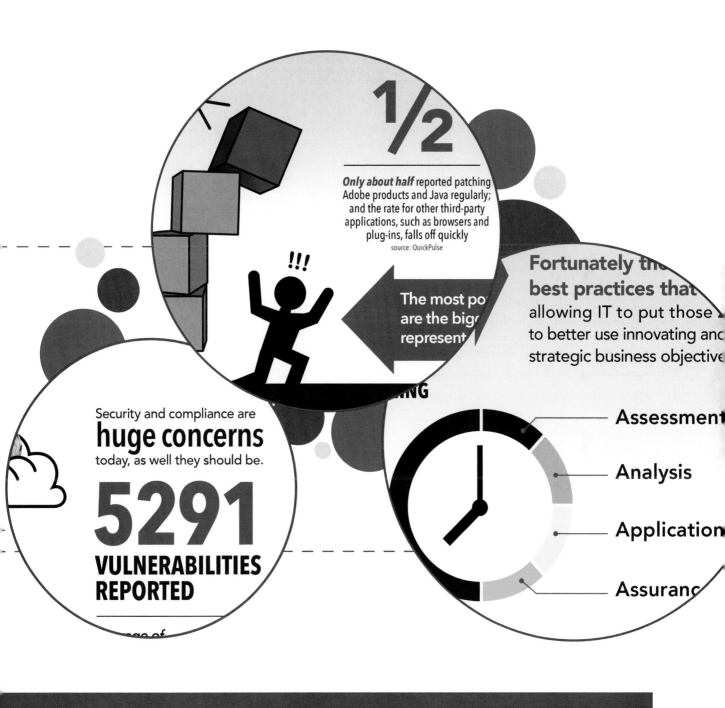

**1/2**

*Only about half* reported patching Adobe products and Java regularly; and the rate for other third-party applications, such as browsers and plug-ins, falls off quickly
source: QuickPulse

The most po
are the big
represent

Fortunately th
best practices that
allowing IT to put those
to better use innovating and
strategic business objective

Security and compliance are
## huge concerns
today, as well they should be.

# 5291
**VULNERABILITIES REPORTED**

Assessment

Analysis

Application

Assuranc

# TECHNOLOGY INDUSTRY VISUAL SOLUTIONS

- Large Computer Hardware Vendor Showcases Benefits of a Converged Infrastructure

- Demonstrating Business Value for Tablets

- Big Data and Social Business

# LARGE COMPUTER HARDWARE VENDOR SHOWCASES BENEFITS OF A CONVERGED INFRASTRUCTURE

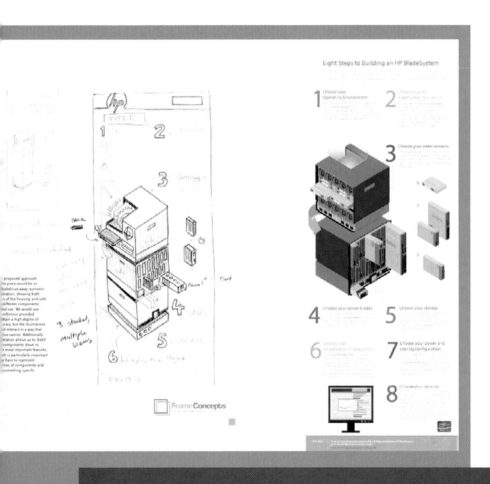

While the eight steps to build a blade server might be intimidating, even for the most technical audience, this infographic leverages a compelling isometric cutaway and bold iconographic and typography, so that the business user can grasp the logic and value of the program. The sample also showcases the pencil ideation exercise that went into the project before the published rendering was created.

# DEMONSTRATING BUSINESS VALUE FOR TABLETS

Conceptually, the tablet does conjure up images of the consumer sitting on a couch surfing the Internet or playing the latest version of Angry Birds. This large tablet vendor wanted to frame things differently and provocatively challenges the read on data-backed as to whether they are realizing untapped business benefits.

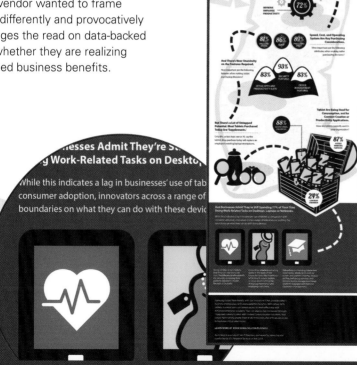

# BIG DATA AND
# SOCIAL BUSINESS

A large technology global solutions provider needed to conceptually show how their new social business solution would have transformative effects on business functions day-to-day. This speculative sketch was an explorative approach to teasing out the value.

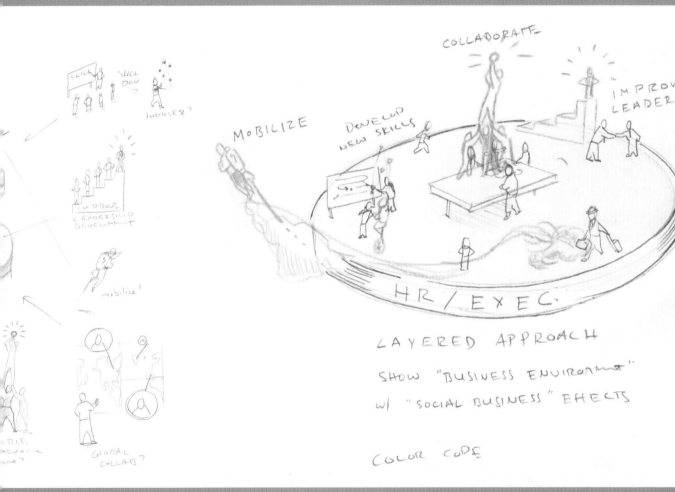

COLLABORATE

IMPROVE LEADERSHIP

MOBILIZE

DEVELOP NEW SKILLS

HR / EXEC.

LAYERED APPROACH

SHOW "BUSINESS ENVIRONMENT"

W/ "SOCIAL BUSINESS" EFFECTS

COLOR CODE

# TELECOMMUNICATIONS INDUSTRY VISUAL SOLUTIONS

- Alaskan Telecommunications Firm Showcases an Engineering Marvel

- Canadian Data Services FIrm Visually Launches Its New Platform of Business Data Services

- Wireless Provider Engages with an Infographic Rich Media Ad

# ALASKAN TELECOMMUNICATIONS FIRM SHOWCASES AN ENGINEERING MARVEL

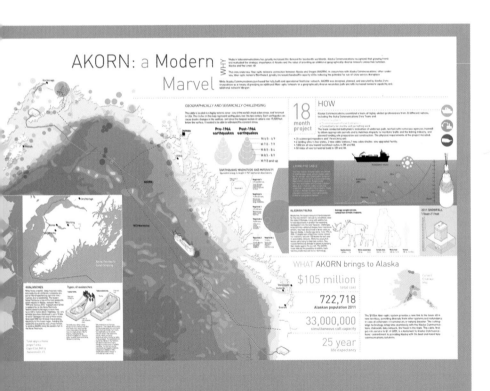

The client had laid cable in a 700-square-mile radius connecting Alaska to Oregon (AKORN project) on one of the most seismically active ocean floors in the world—all of this to deliver new 4G feature and large bandwidth capabilities to its Alaskan customers. To help showcase this impressive feat and what it means to their customers, Frame Concepts created a large poster and then an interactive version so its audience could explore the project and appreciate its significance.

# CANADIAN DATA SERVICES FIRM VISUALLY LAUNCHES ITS NEW PLATFORM OF BUSINESS DATA SERVICES

The client had been busy refining and expanding its new Business Data Services offering and wanted to make sure the benefits it was delivering on launch would not be lost on its customer base and potentially new customers. To accomplish this, a static pictogram and an interactive version to showcase the value was developed showcasing the layers of innovation and value.

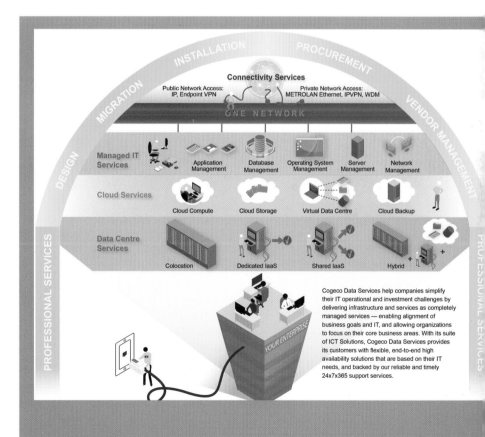

# WIRELESS PROVIDER ENGAGES WITH AN INFOGRAPHIC RICH MEDIA AD

The impact with big data, cloud offerings and proliferation of devices is dealt with an intelligent networking solution as showcased in this clever interactive infographic rich media unit. This innovative online ad approach integrates infographcs with compelling parallax features to significantly improve click-though rate.

TODAY'S BUSINESS ENVIRONMENT IS ABOUT BEING CONNECTED ON ANY PLATFORM OR DEVICE.

But the growing adoption of cloud computing, the explosion of big data, and the mobile revolution are impacting the network.

IT

...GENT NETWORKING SOLU...

...t for companies to align network development initiative... ...te strategies so the network will deliver the right informat... the right people—rapidly.

...S AND POTENTIA...

16%

MUST DEDICATE MORE RESOURCES TO NETWORK SERVICES

...VERIZON PRIV...

CONNECTED LOCATIONS

CONTACT CENTER

> READ HOW INTELLIGENT NETWORK SOLUTIONS CAN HELP YOUR ENTERPRISE

VOICE & VIDEO SOLUTION

REMOTE ACCESS & BACKUP

> READ HOW TO ADVANCE YOUR ENTERPRISE WITH ENTERPRISE SOLUTIONS

# TRAVEL INDUSTRY VISUAL SOLUTIONS

- Large IT Airport Solution Provider Infographic "Facts" Showcases Impressive Numbers and Innovation

- Student Travel Agency Visually Demonstrated Differentiated Value

- Cloud Services in an Airport Industry Context

# LARGE IT AIRPORT SOLUTION PROVIDER INFOGRAPHIC "FACTS" SHOWCASES IMPRESSIVE NUMBERS AND INNOVATION

The client, a world leader in travel IT services, showcased their impressive logistics numbers. Number of passengers, countries, airports, languages, baggage, and technical innovation all served to more than suggest that they deliver tremendous value to the travel industry. This sample also includes the pencil sketches that are an important part of the process to shape the infographic exactly how the client needs it for their particular business goals.

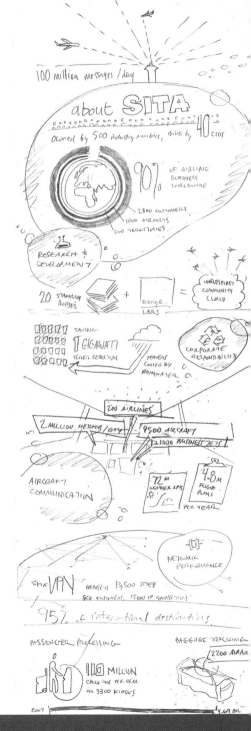

# ONE STEP AHEAD

SITA has operated at the forefront of technology for the air transport industry (ATI) for over 60 years, defining the future of the industry with innovative technology. Read the facts…

## OWNERSHIP

**500** CO-OWNERS FROM MEMBERS OF THE ATI

**40+** ATI CIOs ON SITA'S BOARD AND COUNCIL

ON **20** COMMITTEES TO SET STANDARDS

## GLOBAL PRESENCE

**4,500** EMPLOYEES

**2,800** CUSTOMERS — AIRLINES, AIRPORTS, SERVICES AND GOVERNMENTS

**140** NATIONALITIES

**200** COUNTRIES & TERRITORIES

**70** LANGUAGES SPOKEN

**1,000** AIRPORTS

SITA SUPPORTS ALMOST EVERY AIRLINE AND AIRPORT IN THE WORLD

NEARLY EVERY PASSENGER TRIP RELIES ON OUR TECHNOLOGY

## INNOVATION

**R&D** — INVESTING 5.5% OF REVENUES IN R&D

**PARTNERSHIP** — SITA AND ORANGE BUSINESS SERVICES STARTED A SUCCESSFUL PARTNERSHIP IN 2001

**CLOUD** — FIRST ATI COMMUNITY CLOUD LAUNCHED IN 2011

**MOBILE DATA** — FIRST GLOBAL MOBILE DATA SERVICE BUILT IN 2011

**NFC** — FIRST ATI NFC SOLUTION, SPEEDING PASSENGER ACCESS AND BOARDING VIA NFC-ENABLED SMARTPHONES IN 2012

**FACEBOOK** — FIRST AIRLINE BOOKING ENGINE INTEGRATED WITH FACEBOOK IN 2011

## AWARDS

2011 FROST & SULLIVAN: Airport IT Solutions provider of the year
2011 FROST & SULLIVAN: Global Customer Value Enhancement in **Border Management**
2011 CAPA: IT Innovation of the Year

## NETWORK AND INFRASTRUCTURE

**95%** OF ALL INTERNATIONAL DESTINATIONS COVERED BY SITA'S EXTENSIVE NETWORK

**13,500** AIR TRANSPORT SITES CONNECTED BY SITA VPN NETWORKS

**15,000+** IP CONNECTIONS

### BAGGAGE

**Nº1** BAGGAGE TRACING NETWORK, **WORLDTRACER**, TRACES MILLIONS OF MISHANDLED BAGS WORLDWIDE EACH YEAR

IN USE AT **2,200** AIRPORT LOCATIONS

PLAYED A MAJOR ROLE IN **47%** COST REDUCTION IN MISHANDLED BAGGAGE

**$4.69 BILLION** 2007   **$2.58 BILLION** 2012

## PASSENGERS

**3,300** NETWORKED CHECK-IN KIOSKS

**30,000** CUTE SYSTEMS IN USE WORLDWIDE

**120M** PASSENGERS BOARDED PER YEAR VIA HORIZON SYSTEM

**1.3 BILLION PASSENGERS** HAVE BEEN CHECKED IN USING SITA'S CUTE SYSTEM

## AIRCRAFT

**100** MILLION TYPE B MESSAGES CARRIED PER DAY

**4.8** MILLION FLIGHT PLANS DELIVERED PER YEAR

**72** MILLION WEATHER AND AERONAUTICAL BRIEFS PER YEAR

**12,700** AIRCRAFT USING SITA'S AIRCRAFT COMMUNICATION SERVICES

## CORPORATE SOCIAL RESPONSIBILITY

- SITA HAS SIGNED THE UNITED NATIONS GLOBAL COMPACT
- SITA CURRENTLY SPONSORS 40+ CSR PROJECTS IN 19 COUNTRIES
- SITA IS THE FIRST IT PROVIDER TO SIGN UP TO THE ATI'S COMMITMENT TO ACTION ON CLIMATE CHANGE

THE GLOBAL COMPACT — WE SUPPORT

TO LEARN MORE ABOUT SITA VISIT WWW.SITA.AERO

---

### IP CONNE…

## PASSENGERS

**3,300** NETWORKED CHECK-IN KIOSKS

**30,000** CUTE SYSTEMS IN USE WORLDWIDE

**12…** PAS… PER… HOR…

## 3 BILLION PASSEN…
…EN CHECKED IN USING SITA'S CUTE SYSTEM

**MOBILE DATA** — FIRST GLOBAL MOBILE DATA SERVICE BUILT IN 2011

**NFC** — FIRST ATI NFC SOLUTION, SPEEDING PASSENGER ACCESS AND BOARDING VIA NFC-ENABLED SMARTPHONES IN 2012

**FACEBOOK** — FIRST AIRLINE BOOKING ENGINE INTEGRATED WITH FACEBOOK IN 2011

# STUDENT TRAVEL AGENCY VISUALLY DEMONSTRATED DIFFERENTIATED VALUE

A student-focused travel agency has a tailored solution that thinks of everything for student travel and showcased it in this infographic, each contextualized benefit with a playful meandering travel path and compelling iconography.

We Make It Simple:
Every step of the way, we handle the nitty gritty so you can enjoy a stress-free trip.

We Match Competitors' Prices:
If you find a lower price for your exact tour with another company, we will match the amount. It's that simple!

We Make Payments Easy:
Our flexible payment schedule and collection and billing services allow for 24/7 online access to check account balances and to make credit card payments.

We Plan The Trip You Want:
We help create an experience that specifically fits your needs.

We're the Travel Partner You Can Trust
As a global leader in travel, we keep the promises we make.

Unexpected Expenses Are On Us:
We cover any costs associated with trip-related delays.

Our Relationships Save You Money:
The connections we have with venues, airlines and festivals allow you to get the best value for your trip.

We Provide Medical And Liability Insurance:
We offer the best health and accidental insurance in the industry, with both general and professional coverage.

Your Students Are Safe With Us:
From hotel security to 24-hour on-tour hotline support, we assure the safety and security of your group.

Refunds Are Guaranteed:
In the event of an unforeseen cancellation, your payments are protected when you opt into Refund Guarantee Protection.

# CLOUD SERVICES IN AN AIRPORT INDUSTRY CONTEXT

While the cloud has become commonplace delivery and a technical model for the technology industry, Not so much for the travel industry. This client is a leader in this space and has nuanced cloud-based services to the complete airport travel experience. This infographic metes out the "how" and the "why" in one provocative visual snapshot.

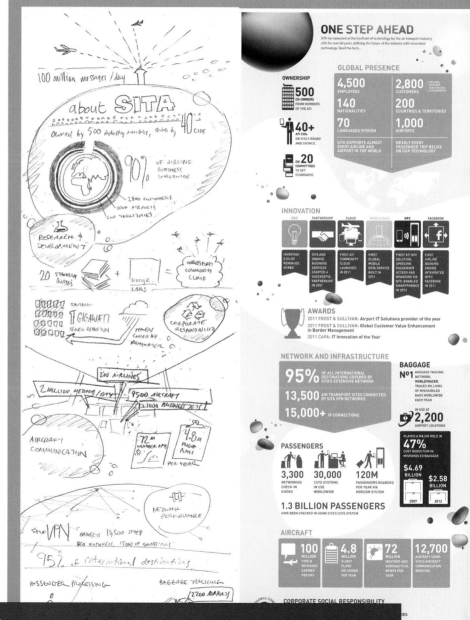

# IN CLOSING: A SOBERING AND A POSITIVE NOTE

# SOBERING NOTE

From personal experience over the last five years, presenting to hundreds of clients, it is very typical to see that the clients' websites and communication materials are not intuitive or engaging and have not been exposed to the information design craft. In 2016 that's a bit sobering, and I assume that some of the arguments against information design are still holding. Quite

often I hear this kind of explanation: "I realize it was a rookie mistake, but I have squandered my entire budget into the solution itself." And they are at the same time frustrated that the marketplace does not understand them or—even worse—does not even care.

Certainly, if any of us do a quick glance at the majority of busi-

nesses' websites and materials, we notice that they are less than to be desired, to put it politely. Typically, when I present a screenshot of their website and materials to a prospect , they do not even argue that they are lacking. There is a pervasive need for visual solutions in business communications.

# POSITIVE NOTE

But if we see that there is a credible argument for visual solutions in business communications, as argued in Part 1 of this book, and that there are tangible and repeatable steps to plan and manage the visual creation process, as shown in Part 2, and then see the incredible breadth of visual solutions in all major industries showcased in Part 3, then we can see the light at the end of the tunnel. If this book enables some organizations to get onboard and realize the benefits of taking a visually centric approach armed with information design, then the goal of this book has been realized.

# EPILOGUE: A CALL TO VISUAL ACTION

For those who have taken the time to go through the arguments and practical visual solution guidance and pored through a myriad of visual case studies, I congratulate you. And I offer this piece of advice: Do not allow anyone to tell you that a dense topic cannot be captured in a visually intuitive and engaging fashion. Humans came up with every idea that is brought to market. It made sense to them. It made sense to investors. It made sense to the founders and management team. All those huddles over a whiteboard and gestures to a noodle on a piece of paper can be visual, starting with a pencil sketch on a piece of a paper. And every business communication application can benefit from visual information design-driven solutions. With the advancements of information design and technical extensions into interactive, data driven visualization, integrated film, and application development, there is simply no reason not to engage your audience visually, however they like to consume information.

Time for you to get started! Everything starts with blank paper and a pencil. Your visual engagement adventure—and success—are ready for you to begin. You are only a sketch away.

# INDEX

departments financial ROI visualization, 222–223; dashboard on the financials of IT security, 209; financial data firm's Small Business Health Index report, 293; financial information databases infographic, 118–119; innovation lab's new financial data-driven, 251; insurance brokers showcasing their membership numbers, 234–235; movie industry showcasing new financing model, 158–159; new trading communication platform, 232; ship analogy of financial forecasting infographic, 302–303; showcasing financial data innovation with infographic series, 174; storyboarding finance new credit approval process, 250; visualizing benefits of bank vs. a credit union, 233

Financial (or luxury) argument, 61

Frame Concepts: infographic animations used at, 84; scoping sketch turned to vector art at, 73; taking clients through relevant visual samples at, 72, 73; visually centric solutions used by, 2, 3. *See also* Information design agencies; *specific visual*

Full render visuals: animation artwork, 102; description and creation of, 96; Nuclear Reactor Spare Parts Visualization, 105

## G

Graphic design: description of the task of, 40; information design vs., 40

Green energy. *See* Energy industrial visual solutions

## H

Hardware provider's data-driven virtualization, 196–197

Healthcare industry visual solutions: category of, 115; dental kits distribution visualization, 241; managed healthcare provider's training game visual, 153, 178, 240; new community-based delivery model visual, 238–239

HP BladeSystem program, 310

HR and recruiting industry visual solutions: category of, 115; pharmaceutical merger visualized into improved employee experience, 247, 276–277; social and mobile recruiting using interactive and visual solution, 144, 244–245; social employee referral program visual, 246; social media recruitment platform for sales department, 204

## I

Iconography: children and widow charitable organization's use of, 168; college athletic department ROI visualization using, 222–223; demonstrating differentiated value of student-focused travel agency, 324; dental kits distribution visualization, 241;

enterprise software vendor showcasing productivity in cloud, 304–305; financial data firm's Small Business Health Index report, 293; hardware vendor showcasing benefits of converged infrastructure, 310; insurance brokers association's membership numbers visual using, 234–235; reputation consultancy visualizing results against bottom line using, 264; small business health index infographic leveraging, 128–129; social employee referral program, 246; technical writing use of, 77, 83

Ideation phase: evaluating an information design agency's, 85; pencil sketches used during, 35, 41, 43, 46, 91–93, 252–253

Ideation/product development: collaborative tool going through visual phase of, 252–253; innovation lab's new financial data-driven visual solutions,

251; storyboarding finance new credit approval process, 250; visual product brochure on new product release, 205; visual solutions for, 115. *See also* Product development and programmers

Illustration: description of the task of, 41; information design vs., 41

Inbound content marketing: the rise of inbound and, 51; scoping pencil sketch on strategies for, 110–111; understanding the importance of, 26–30; as visual application category, 114. *See also* Business communication; Sales and marketing profession visual solutions

Inbound marketing programs: health index iconic design integrated with infographic content, 128–129; networking vendor visual strategy for their differentiated offering, 126; reputation consultancy strategy for existing clients, 127

Independent film platform pictogram, 272

Infographic designer community sites, 77, 80

Infographic freelancers, 77, 79

Infographic options: ad agency, 77, 82; animated "explainer" video shops, 77, 84; community site of infographic designers, 77, 80; infographic freelancers, 77, 79; do-it-yourself tools, 77, 78; technical writers, 77, 83; traditional marketing or PR agency, 77, 81

Infographics: airport infographic "facts" showcasing numbers and innovation, 322–323; on best practices for new construction network deployment, 290–291; on California credit union name change, 191; client visualization using animated video with, 133; on cloud services in context of an airport industry, 325; demonstrating differentiated value of student-focused travel agency, 324; ecommerce metrics during ad week, 120–121, 270–271, 296–297; financial information databases, 118–119; financial services showcasing data innovation with series of, 174; green energy startup's, 215, 227; health index iconic design integrated with, 128–129; how tables are reinventing retail customer experience, 298; improving prescription delivery with tablets, 278–279; for meeting software platform on meeting inefficiencies, 157; networking vendor visualizing best practices for setting up network, 258–259; new allergy over-the-counter drug interactive, 280–281; of nonprofit architectural association to show community value, 169, 285; predictive analytics firm debriefing analysts visually using, 122–123, 256–257; for SEO agency on driving their client's traffic, 162–163; ship analogy of financial forecasting, 302–303; software vendor's three-part series of, 194–195; vendors and other options for, 77–78; Verizon's Intelligent Networking showcased using interactive, 318–319; as visual application category, 114; *Wall Street Journal* blog and online real estate, 190; *Wall Street Journal* Trick-Or-Treating infographic goes viral, 216–217. *See also* Animated infographic videos

Information design: graphic design vs., 40; how it works, 59; illustration vs., 41; the ingredients and tasks of, 43–45; insurance broker membership visualization and, 234–235; leveraging for business communications, 50–53; pencil sketch ideation phase of, 35, 41, 43, 46; technical communication vs., 42; why it is a good business communication solution, 48

Information design agencies, 85. *See also* Frame Concepts

Information design teams: full render passed to a rendering team from the, 96; full renders by the, 96; partial renders by the, 94–95; pencil sketches for ideation with your, 35, 41, 43, 46, 91–93

Information economy, 29, 32

Information overload, 29, 31

Insurance broker membership visualization, 234–235

Interactive media visual category, 114

Interactive solution pictograms: animated infographic video as extension of the, 70; branding agency's iPad timeline data visualization, 165; Canadian firm launching business data services in static and, 317; construction field software startup's tablet vs. tables, 145, 214; on data reconciliation offering, 186; extending from the static to, 97; increasing website visitor engagement with an, 52; large construction projects software engaging with, 156; to show competency gaps of trading analysts, 179; social and mobile recruiting using, 144, 244–245; starting your approach to visual content marketing with the, 68; storyboard for, 98–99; trading communications platform, 146, 232; value proposition exhibited on your, 68, 69, 70, 71; as visual application category, 114. *See also* Pictograms

iPads. *See* Tablets

IT networking industry visual solutions: IT network data visualization for CIOs, 260–261; networking vendor visualizing best practices for setting up network, 258–259; predictive analytics firm debriefing analysts visually, 122–123, 256–257; value proposition on performance monitoring, 175; visual solutions for the, 115

## K

Kickoff meetings: concept sketch for ideation during, 91–93; the end goal of, 91

## L

Lievens, Tamara, 141
Lifecycle of a trade solution pictogram, 138
Literacy learning visual, 220
Luxury (or financial) argument for visuals, 61

## M

Managed healthcare provider training game visual, 153, 178, 240
Management consulting industry visual solutions: category of, 115; pictogram of marketing automation process, 164, 266–267, 284; reputation consultancy visualizing results against bottom

line, 264; visualization of new corporate performance model, 265, 292
Marketing agencies, 77, 81
Marketing. *See* Inbound content marketing; Sales and marketing visual solutions
Media: the audience familiarity with visual communication in, 50; as increasingly visual, 29, 37; the "luxury" of, 61; visual category of interactive, 114. *See also* Television
Media industry visual solutions: communicating ecommerce metrics during ad week, 120–121, 270–271, 296–297; independent film platform startup's use of pictogram, 272; new user interface integrating TV and online metrics, 273. *See also* Social media/PR visual solutions
Meeting software infographic, 157
Metropolitan College of New York, 2
Movie industry's new financing model, 158–159

clients of your, 93; sales tools indicated on the, 71; starting to communicate value proposition in your, 68, 69; turned into a spaghetti slide, 20; turned into vector art, 72–73; used to get everyone onboard, 72; various examples during the ideation phase, 35, 41, 43, 46, 88, 91–93, 252–253; visual solutions to your organization, 110–111. *See also* Pencil sketches

Pension fund security costs, 209

Pharmaceutical industry visual solutions: improving prescription delivery with tablets infographic, 278–279; interactive infographic on new allergy over-the-counter drug, 280–281; merger visualized into improved employee experience, 247, 276–277; as visual solutions category, 115

Pictograms: Canadian firm launching business data services in interactive and static, 317; independent film platform

startup's use of, 272; lifecycle of a trade, 138; marketing automation process, 164, 266–267, 284; shipping network, 140–141; on telecommunications' new platform of integrated data services, 184–185; video analytics firm's real-time sports signage on audience awareness, 139; as visual application category, 114. *See also* Interactive solution pictograms

PowerPoint "spaghetti" slides, 19, 20

PR. *See* Social media/PR visual solutions

Product development and programmers: dynamically visualizing nuclear spare parts, 208; visual dashboard on financials of IT security, 209; as visual solutions category, 115. *See also* Ideation/product development

Professional services industry visual solutions: category

of, 115; infographic showing Architecture Association's community value, 169, 285; iPad dynamic visualization of CPA organization's anniversary, 152, 286–287; visualizing marketing automation process, 164, 266–267, 284

Programming visual solutions, 115

Psychological argument for visuals, 57

**R**

Real estate industry. *See* Construction and real estate industry visual solutions

Recruiting. *See* HR and recruiting industry visual solutions

Reputation consultancy: inbound marketing program of, 127; visual for marketing insight workshop of, 202–203; visualizing results against bottom line of, 264

Research industry visual solutions: category of, 115; energy savings research visualization, 198–199; enterprise software vendor's three-part infographic series, 194–195; financial data firm's Small Business Health Index report, 293; hardware provider's client data-driven virtualization journey, 196–197; infographic on best practices for new construction network deployment, 290–291; management consulting firm's new corporate performance model, 265, 292

Retail and ecommerce industry visual solutions: category of, 115; ecommerce metrics infographics during ad week, 120–121, 270–271, 296–297; how tables are reinventing retail customer experience, 298

## S

Sales and marketing profession visual solutions: category of, 115; marketing automation consultancy pictogram, 164, 266–267, 284; marketing metric argument for visuals, 58; marketing reputation consultancy's insight workshop, 202–203; showing transition to solution from product for sales training, 180–181; social media recruitment platform, 204; visual product brochure on new product release, 205. *See also* Inbound content marketing

Sales tools: indicated on the scoping pencil sketch, 71; organizing your company's, 71

Scoping pencil sketches. *See* Pencil sketches

Security industry visual solutions: costs of pension fund security, 209; security software vendor on patch management, 306–307; visual dashboard on financials of IT security, 209

SEO agency's infographic, 162–163

Ship analogy of financial forecasting infographic, 302–303

Shipping network solution pictogram, 140–141

Silicon Valley, 2

Sketches: coexistence of pencil and partial render, 95; of collaborative tool going through visual ideation phase, 252–253; data-driven visualization pencil, 103–104; for ideation during the kickoff meeting, 91–93; red flags on inadequate review by clients of your, 93; scoping pencil, 20, 35, 41, 43, 46, 66–73

Social media/PR visual solutions: category of, 115; interactive media applications for, 114; for name change by California credit union, 191; online real estate on *Wall Street Journal* blog, 190; recruitment platform for sales department, 204; social and mobile recruiting using interactive and visual solution, 144, 244–245; social employee referral program, 246. *See also* Media industry visual solutions

demonstrating business value for tablets, 311; enterprise software vendor showcasing productivity in cloud, 304–305; hardware provider's client data-driven virtualization journey, 196–197; hardware vendor showcasing benefits of converged infrastructure, 310; meeting software platform's infographic on meeting inefficiencies, 157; security software vendor showing patch management approach, 306–307; ship analogy of financial forecasting infographic, 302–303; software vendor's three-part infographic series, 194–195; video analytics firm's real-time sports signage pictogram, 139; as visual solutions category, 115

Telecommunications industry visual solutions: Alaskan to Oregon (AKORN project) engineering marvel, 316; Canadian firm launching business data services, 317; interactive infographic on Verizon's Intelligent Networking, 318–319; lifecycle of a trade solution pictogram, 138; visual of new platform of integrated data services, 184–185; visual solutions for the, 115

Television: new user interface integrating TV and online metrics, 273; television metrics dashboard, 210; visualization on social effect of Super Bowl ads on, 187, 299. *See also* Media

Trading communications platform interactive pictogram, 146, 232

Traffic analogy of data management research video, 134–135

Training visual solutions: lessons learning on using, 13; managed healthcare provider's interactive training game visual, 153, 178, 240; pictogram used to show competency gaps, 179; showing transition to solution from product for sales, 180–181; as visual solutions category, 115

Travel industry visual solutions: airport infographic "facts" showcasing numbers and innovation, 322–323; category of, 115; demonstrating differentiated value of student-focused travel agency, 324; infographic on cloud services in context of an airport industry, 325

Trick-Or-Treating infographic, 216–217

## U

University of Western Ontario, 2
*USA Today,* 50

## V

Value proposition: animated infographic video showing your, 68, 69, 70, 71; as having become the norm, 53; interactive solution pictogram showing your, 68, 69, 70, 71; lesson on corporate training, 13; network performance monitoring's visualization showing, 175; scoop sketch on your approach to visual solutions and, 66–67, 68–69; scoping pencil sketches used to communicate your, 68, 69; visual of tablet's, 311

Value proposition videos: animated infographic video as, 68, 69, 70–71; as visual application category, 114

Vector art, 72–73

Vender management: animation, 97, 100–102; concept sketch: ideation begins, 88, 91–93; for creativity within your timelines, 88; data-driven visualization process, 97, 103–105; full render, 96; interactive, 97, 98–99; learn to love the pencil for editing, 88, 89; partial render, 94–95; pre-delivery: the outline, 88, 90

Vender options: ad agency, 79, 82; animated "explainer" video shop, 77, 84; community site of infographic designers, 77, 80; do-it-yourself tools, 77, 78; evaluating information design agencies to provide you with, 85; infographic freelancer, 77, 79; technical writers, 77, 83; traditional, 76; traditional marketing or PR agency, 79, 81

Venders: evaluating information design agencies, 85; managing, 88–105; options for, 79–84

Verizon's Intelligent Networking interactive infographic, 318–319

Video analytics firms: pictogram on detecting real-time sports signage delivery, 139; Super Bowl data visualization by, 187, 299

Videos: client visualization using infographic bonus with animated, 133; creating and media channels of your animated, 68; "hot" marketing strategy of animated, 70; software vendor's data management animation, 132; traffic analogy of data management research findings, 134–135; value proposition exhibited on your animated, 68, 69, 70–71; visual application category of animated, 114

Visual-centric solution arguments: examining the, 56; information design works, 59; the marketing metric, 58; opposing the financial (or luxury), 61; the organic, 60; the psychological, 57

Visual-centric solutions: applications to your organization, 66–73; examining the feasibility of, 2, 3; as having become the norm, 53; increasingly used in media consumption, 37; making the argument for, 56–61; positive note on business communication, 329; reasons for effectiveness in business communications, 56–61; tracing the author's journey in using, 10–21; visualizing the options for vendors and different, 76–84; why information design is a good, 48. *See also specific category*